Introduction to

Metadata

Second Edition

Edited by Murtha Baca

The Getty Research Institute

© 2008 J. Paul Getty Trust
Second Edition, 2008
Version 3.0

Published by the Getty Research Institute, Los Angeles
Getty Publications
1200 Getty Center Drive, Suite 500
Los Angeles, CA 90049-1682
www.gettypublications.org
Gregory M. Britton, *Publisher*

The Getty Research Institute Publications Program
Thomas Gaehtgens, *Director, Getty Research Institute*
Gail Feigenbaum, *Associate Director, Programs*
Julia Bloomfield, *Head, Publications Program*

Introduction to Metadata
Second Edition
Murtha Baca, *Series Editor*
Patrick E. Pardo, *Project Editor*
Sheila U. Berg, *Manuscript Editor*
Elizabeth Zozom, *Production Coordinator*
Designed by Hespenheide Design, Newbury Park, California
Printed and bound by Odyssey Press Inc.

Library of Congress Cataloging-in-Publication Data
Introduction to metadata / edited by Murtha Baca. — 2nd ed.
    p. cm.
 Includes bibliographical references.
 ISBN 978-0-89236-896-9 (pbk.)
1. Database management. 2. Metadata. 3. World Wide Web.
4. Information organization. I. Baca, Murtha. II. Getty Research Institute.
 QA76.9.D3I599 2008
 025.3—dc22
                                        2008007871

Reader's Note: The editor and authors
of this publication are aware that the
noun "metadata" (like the noun "data") is
plural and, therefore, should take a plural
verb form. However, in order to avoid
awkward locutions, it has been treated here
throughout as singular.

This volume was published in September
2008. Updated print editions will be
offered periodically. An online version of
this edition is also available at:
www.getty.edu/research/
conducting_research/standards/
intrometadata

Contents

Introduction

Murtha Baca

Like metadata itself, the realm of online resources is constantly and rapidly evolving. Much has changed in the digital information landscape since the first print edition of this book was published in 1998 and the revised online version appeared in 2000. The time is right for an updated edition of this text, intended to give a general introduction to metadata and to explain some of the key tools, concepts, and issues associated with using metadata to build authoritative, reliable, and useful digital resources.

Metadata creation is—or should often be—a collaborative effort, as is this book. For this edition, the three contributors to the 2000 version wrote updated chapters, and I was fortunate to find a new contributor to address the crucial issue of rights metadata.

In the first chapter, Anne Gilliland provides an overview of metadata—its types, roles, and characteristics—as well as facts about metadata that belie several common misconceptions. She also addresses current trends in metadata, especially that of metadata created by users rather than trained information professionals. Activities such as social tagging, social bookmarking, and the resulting forms of user-created metadata such as "folksonomies" are playing an increasingly important role in the realm of digital information.

In the second chapter, Tony Gill discusses metadata as it relates to resources on the Web. He explains how Web search engines work and how they use metadata, data, links, and relevance ranking to help users find what they are seeking and discusses in detail the commercial search engine that as of this writing has dominated the Web for several years: Google. He explains the difference between the Visible Web and the Hidden Web and the important implications and issues relating to making resources reachable from commercial, publicly available search engines versus systems that have one or more "barriers" to access—because they are fee based or password protected or require a particular IP address, or simply because they are not technically exposed to commercial search engines. Gill also raises issues relating to open access to digitized materials and legal obstacles that currently prevent open access to many materials.

In the third chapter, Mary Woodley examines the methods, tools, standards, and protocols that can be used to publish and disseminate digital collections in a variety of online venues. She shows how "seamless searching"—integrated access to a variety of resources residing in different information systems and formulated according to a range of standard and nonstandard metadata schemes—is still far from a reality. Woodley contrasts the method of "federation" by means of the building of union catalogs of digital collections by aggregating metadata records from diverse contributors into a single database with metasearching—real-time searching of diverse resources that have not been aggregated but rather are searched in situ by means of one or more protocols. Each method requires specific skills and knowledge; particular procedures, protocols, and data standards; and the appropriate technical infrastructure. Creating union resources via physical aggregation of metadata records or via metadata harvesting is a good thing, but we should keep in mind that it does not necessarily solve the Hidden Web problem enunciated by Gill. If resources are publicly available but users cannot reach them from Google, instead having to find the specific search page for the particular union resource, we cannot say that we have provided unfettered access to that resource. Woodley also stresses the importance of data value standards—controlled vocabularies, thesauri, lists of terms and names, and folksonomies—for enhancing end-user access. She points out that mapping of metadata elements alone is not sufficient to connect all users with what they seek; the data values, that is, the vocabularies used to populate those elements, should also be mapped.

Maureen Whalen's new chapter, "Rights Metadata Made Simple," argues that the research and capture of standards-based rights metadata should be core activities of memory institutions and offers practical, realistic options for determining and recording core rights metadata. If institutions would commit the effort and resources to following Whalen's advice, many of the legal obstacles mentioned by Gill in his discussion of libraries and the Web could be surmounted.

In another new section in this edition, "Practical Principles for Metadata Creation and Maintenance," we again emphasize that institutions need to change old paradigms and procedures. They need to make a lasting commitment to creating and continually updating the various types of core metadata relating to their collections and the digital surrogates of collection materials that we all seem to be in such a hurry to create.

Our slim volume concludes with a glossary and a selected bibliography. The glossary is not intended to be comprehensive; rather, its purpose is to explain the key concepts and tools discussed in this book. The bibliography, too, is deliberately restricted to a few relevant publications and resources. The footnotes in each of the chapters provide numerous additional references to publications and online resources relevant to the topic of metadata and digital libraries.

At the end of her chapter, Gilliland compares metadata to an investment that, if wisely managed, can deliver a significant return on intellectual capital. I would venture to expand on her financial metaphor and say that metadata is one of our most important assets. Hardware and software come and go—sometimes becoming obsolete with alarming rapidity—but high-quality, standards-based, system-independent metadata can be used, reused, migrated, and disseminated in any number of ways, even in ways that we cannot anticipate at this moment.

Digitization does not equal access. The mere act of creating digital copies of collection materials does not make those materials findable, understandable, or utilizable to our ever-expanding audience of online users. But digitization combined with the creation of carefully crafted metadata can significantly enhance end-user access; and our users are the primary reason that we create digital resources.

Setting the Stage

Anne J. Gilliland

Metadata, literally "data about data," has become a widely used yet still frequently underspecified term that is understood in different ways by the diverse professional communities that design, create, describe, preserve, and use information systems and resources. It is a construct that has been around for as long as humans have been organizing information, albeit transparently in many cases, and today we create and interact with it in increasingly digital ways. For the past hundred years at least, the creation and management of metadata has primarily been the responsibility of information professionals engaged in cataloging, classification, and indexing; but as information resources are increasingly put online by the general public, metadata considerations are no longer solely the province of information professionals. Although *metadata* is arguably a much less familiar term among creators and consumers of networked digital content who are not information professionals per se, these same individuals are increasingly adept at creating, exploiting, and assessing user-contributed metadata such as Web page title tags, folksonomies, and social bookmarks. Schoolchildren and college students are taught in information literacy programs to look for metadata such as provenance and date information in order to ascertain the authoritativeness of information that they retrieve on the Web. Thus it has become more important than ever that not only information professionals but also other creators and users of digital content understand the critical roles of different types of metadata in ensuring accessible, authoritative, interoperable, scaleable, and preservable cultural heritage information and record-keeping systems.

Until the mid-1990s, *metadata* was a term used primarily by communities involved with the management and interoperability of geospatial data and with data management and systems design and maintenance in general. For these communities, *metadata* referred to a suite of industry or disciplinary standards as well as additional internal and external documentation and other data necessary for the identification, representation, interoperability, technical management, performance, and use of data contained in an information system.

Perhaps a more useful, "big picture" way of thinking about metadata is as the sum total of what one can say about any *information object* at any level of aggregation.[1] In this context, an information object is anything that can be addressed and manipulated as a discrete entity by a human being or an information system. The object may comprise a single item, it may be an aggregate of many items, or it may be the entire database or record-keeping system. Indeed, in any given instance one can expect to find metadata relevant to any information object existing simultaneously at the item, aggregation, and system levels.

In general, all information objects, regardless of the physical or intellectual form they take, have three features—content, context, and structure—all of which can and should be reflected through metadata.

- *Content* relates to what the object contains or is about and is *intrinsic* to an information object.
- *Context* indicates the who, what, why, where, and how aspects associated with the object's creation and is *extrinsic* to an information object.
- *Structure* relates to the formal set of associations within or among individual information objects and can be *intrinsic* or *extrinsic* or both.

Cultural heritage information professionals such as museum registrars, library catalogers, and archival processors often apply the term *metadata* to the value-added information that they create to arrange, describe, track, and otherwise enhance access to information objects and the physical collections related to those objects. Such metadata is frequently governed by community-developed and community-fostered standards and best practices in order to ensure quality, consistency, and interoperability. The following Typology of Data Standards organizes these standards into categories and provides examples of each. Markup languages such as HTML and XML provide a standardized way to structure and express these standards for machine processing, publication, and implementation.

Library metadata development has been first and foremost about providing intellectual and physical access to collection materials. *Library metadata* includes indexes, abstracts, and bibliographic records created according to cataloging rules (data content standards) such as the *Anglo-*

---

[1] An information object is a digital item or group of items, regardless of type or format, that can be addressed or manipulated as a single object by a computer. This concept can be confusing in that it can be used to refer both to digital "surrogates" of original objects or items (e.g., digitized images of works of art or material culture, a PDF of an entire book) and to descriptive records relating to objects and/or collections (e.g., catalog records or finding aids).

Table 1. **A Typology of Data Standards**

Type	Examples
Data *structure* standards (metadata element sets, schemas). These are "categories" or "containers" of data that make up a record or other information object.	The set of MARC (Machine-Readable Cataloging format) fields, Encoded Archival Description (EAD), Dublin Core Metadata Element Set (DCMES), Categories for the Description of Works of Art (CDWA), VRA Core Categories
Data *value* standards (controlled vocabularies, thesauri, controlled lists). These are the terms, names, and other values that are used to populate data structure standards or metadata element sets.	Library of Congress Subject Headings (LCSH), Library of Congress Name Authority File (LCNAF), LC Thesaurus for Graphic Materials (TGM), Medical Subject Headings (MeSH), Art & Architecture Thesaurus (AAT), Union List of Artist Names (ULAN), Getty Thesaurus of Geographic Names (TGN), ICONCLASS
Data *content* standards (cataloging rules and codes). These are guidelines for the format and syntax of the data values that are used to populate metadata elements.	Anglo-American Cataloguing Rules (AACR), Resource Description and Access (RDA), International Standard Bibliographic Description (ISBD), Cataloging Cultural Objects (CCO), Describing Archives: A Content Standard (DACS)
Data *format/technical interchange* standards (metadata standards expressed in machine-readable form). This type of standard is often a manifestation of a particular data structure standard (type 1 above), encoded or marked up for machine processing.	MARC21, MARCXML, EAD XML DTD, METS, MODS, CDWA Lite XML schema, Simple Dublin Core XML schema, Qualified Dublin Core XML schema, VRA Core 4.0 XML schema

Note: This table is based on the typology of data standards articulated by Karim Boughida, "CDWA Lite for Cataloging Cultural Objects (CCO): A New XML Schema for the Cultural Heritage Community," in *Humanities, Computers and Cultural Heritage: Proceedings of the XVI International Conference of the Association for History and Computing:* 14–17 (September 2005) (Amsterdam: Royal Netherlands Academy of Arts and Sciences, 2005). Available at http://www.knaw.nl/publicaties/pdf/20051064.pdf.

American Cataloguing Rules (AACR) and data structure standards such as the MARC (*Machine-Readable Cataloging*) format, as well as data value standards such as the *Library of Congress Subject Headings* (LCSH) or the *Art & Architecture Thesaurus* (AAT). Such bibliographic metadata has been systematically and cooperatively created and shared since the 1960s and made available to repositories and users through automated systems such as bibliographic utilities, online public access catalogs (OPACs), and commercially available databases. Today this type of metadata is created not only by humans but also in automated ways through such means as metadata mining, metadata harvesting, and Web crawling. Automation of metadata will inevitably continue to expand with the development of the Resource Description Framework (RDF) and the Semantic Web, which are discussed later in this book.

A large component of archival and museum metadata creation activities has traditionally been focused on context. Elucidating and preserving context is what assists with identifying and preserving the evidential value of records and artifacts in and over time; it is what facilitates the authentication of those objects, and it is what assists researchers with their analysis and interpretation. *Archival and manuscript metadata* (more commonly referred to as *archival description*) includes accession records, finding aids, and catalog records. Archival data structure standards that have been developed in the past three decades include the MARC Archival and Manuscripts Control (AMC) format, published by the Library of Congress in 1984 (now integrated into the MARC21 format for bibliographic description); the General International Standard Archival Description (ISAD (G)), published by the International Council on Archives in 1994; Encoded Archival Description (EAD), adopted as a standard by the Society of American Archivists (SAA) in 1999, and its companion data content standard, *Describing Archives: A Content Standard* (DACS), first published in 2004. The *Metadata Encoding and Transmission Standard* (METS), developed by the Digital Library Federation and maintained by the Library of Congress, is increasingly being used for encoding descriptive, administrative, and structural metadata and digital surrogates at the item level for objects such as digitized photographs, maps, and correspondence from the collections described by finding aids and other collection- or group-level metadata records. While archival metadata was primarily only available locally at individual repositories until the late 1990s, it is now distributed online through resources such as OCLC (Online Computer Library Center),[2] Archives USA,[3] and EAD-based resources such as the Online Archive of California and the Library of Congress's American Memory Project.[4]

Consensus and collaboration have been slower to build in the museum community, where the benefits of standardization of description such as shared cataloging and exchange of descriptive data were less readily apparent until relatively recently. Since the late 1990s, tools such as *Categories for the Description of Works of Art* (CDWA), Spectrum, the CIDOC Conceptual Reference Model, *Cataloging Cultural Objects* (CCO), and the CDWA Lite XML schema have begun to be considered and implemented by museums. Initiatives such as Museums and the Online Archive of California (MOAC)[5] have examined the applicability and extensibility of descriptive standards developed by archives and libraries such as EAD and METS to museum holdings in order to address the integration of cultural information across repository types, as well as the educational needs of users visiting online museum resources.

Although it would seem to be a desirable goal to integrate materials of different types that are related by provenance or subject but distributed across museum, archives, and library repositories, initiatives such as MOAC have met with only limited success. As MOAC and the

---

[2] http://www.oclc.org/.

[3] http://archives.chadwyck.com/.

[4] http://www.oac.cdlib.org/ and http://memory.loc.gov/ammem/index.html.

[5] http://www.bampfa.berkeley.edu/moac/.

mid-1980s development of the now-defunct MARC AMC format have demonstrated, the distinctiveness of the various professional and object-based approaches (e.g., widely differing notions of provenance and collectivity as well as of structure) and the different institutional cultures have left many professionals feeling that their practices and needs have been shoehorned into structures that were developed by another community with quite different practices and users. As enunciated in Principle 6 of "Practical Principles for Metadata Creation and Maintenance" (p. 72), there is no single metadata standard that is adequate for describing all types of collections and materials; selection of the most appropriate suite of metadata standards and tools, and creation of clean, consistent metadata according to those standards, not only will enable good descriptions of specific collection materials but also will make it possible to map metadata created according to different community-specific standards, thus furthering the goal of interoperability discussed in subsequent chapters of this book.

An emphasis on the structure of information objects in metadata development by these communities has perhaps been less overt. However, structure has always been important in information organization and representation, even before computerization. Documentary and publication forms have evolved into industry standards and societal norms and have become an almost transparent information management tool. For example, when users access a birth certificate they can predict its likely structure and content. When academics use a scholarly monograph, they understand intuitively that it will be organized with a table of contents, chapter headings, and an index. Archivists use the physical structure of their finding aids to provide visual cues to researchers about the structural relationships between different parts of a record series or manuscript collection. Archival description also exploits the hierarchical arrangement of records according to the bureaucratic hierarchies and business practices of the creators of those records. However, in recent years there has been increasing criticism that while valuable for retaining context and original order, collection-level, hierarchical metadata as exemplified in archival finding aids privileges the scholarly user of the archive (and those who are familiar with the structure and function of archival finding aids) while leaving the nonexpert user baffled, as well as unnecessarily perpetuating a paper-based descriptive paradigm.[6] In the online world, multiple descriptive relationships between objects can be supported simultaneously, and some of these may more effectively support new types of users and uses in

---

[6] Anne J. Gilliland-Swetland, "Popularizing the Finding Aid: Exploiting EAD to Enhance Online Browsing and Retrieval in Archival Information Systems by Diverse User Groups," *Journal of Internet Cataloging* 4, nos. 3–4 (2001): 199–225.

an environment that is not mediated by a reference archivist. Archives and other collecting institutions are beginning to explore methods of description that exploit item-level metadata for digitized objects so that users can search for specific items, navigate through a collection "bottom-up" as well as "top-down," and collate related collection materials through lateral searching across collections and repositories.

The role of structure has been growing as computer-processing capabilities become increasingly powerful and sophisticated. Information communities are aware that the more highly structured an information object is, the more that structure can be exploited for searching, manipulation, and interrelating with other information objects. Capturing, documenting, and enforcing that structure, however, can only occur if supported by specific types of metadata. In short, in an environment where a user can gain unmediated access to information objects over a network, metadata

- certifies the authenticity and degree of completeness of the content;
- establishes and documents the context of the content;
- identifies and exploits the structural relationships that exist within and between information objects;
- provides a range of intellectual access points for an increasingly diverse range of users; and
- provides some of the information that an information professional might have provided in a traditional, in-person reference or research setting.

But there is more to metadata than description and resource discovery. A more inclusive conceptualization of metadata is needed as we consider the range of activities that may be incorporated into digital information systems. Repositories also create metadata relating to the administration, accessioning, preservation, and use of collections. Acquisition records, exhibition catalogs, licensing agreements, and educational metadata are all examples of these other kinds of metadata and data. Integrated information resources such as virtual museums, digital libraries, and archival information systems include digital versions of actual collection content (sometimes referred to as *digital surrogates*), as well as descriptions of that content (i.e., descriptive metadata, in a variety of formats). Incorporating other types of metadata into such resources reaffirms the importance of metadata in administering collections and maintaining their intellectual integrity both in and over time. Paul Conway alludes to this capability of metadata when he discusses the impact of digitization on preservation:

The digital world transforms traditional preservation concepts from protecting the physical integrity of the object to specifying the creation and maintenance of the object whose intellectual integrity is its primary characteristic.[7]

When applied outside the original repository, the term *metadata* acquires an even broader scope. An Internet resource provider might use *metadata* to refer to information that is encoded in HTML META tags for the purposes of making a Web site easier to find. Individuals who are digitizing images might think of metadata as the information they enter into a header field for the digital file to record information about the image file, the imaging process, and image rights. A social science data archivist might use the term to refer to the systems and research documentation necessary to run and interpret a magnetic tape containing raw research data. An electronic records archivist might use the term to refer to all the contextual, processing, preservation, and use information needed to identify and document the scope, authenticity, and integrity of an active or archival record in an electronic record-keeping or archival preservation system. Metadata is crucial in personal information management and for ensuring effective information retrieval and accountability in record keeping—something that is becoming increasingly important with the rise of electronic commerce and the use of digital content and tools by governments. In all these diverse interpretations, metadata not only identifies and describes an information object; it also documents how that object behaves, its function and use, its relationship to other information objects, and how it should be and has been managed over time.

As this discussion suggests, theory and practices vary considerably due to the differing professional and cultural missions of museums, archives, libraries, and other information and record-keeping communities. Information professionals have a bewildering array of metadata standards and approaches from which to choose. Many highly detailed metadata standards have been developed by individual communities (e.g., MARC, EAD, the Australian Recordkeeping Metadata Schema, RKMS, and some of the standards for Geographic Information Systems) that attempt to articulate their mission-specific differences as well as to facilitate mapping between common data elements. If used appropriately and to their fullest extent, these standards have the potential to create extremely rich metadata that would provide detailed documentation of record-keeping creation and

---

[7] Paul Conway, *Preservation in the Digital World* (Washington, DC: Commission on Preservation and Access, 1996). http://www.clir.org/pubs/reports/conway2/index.html.

[8] Sue McKemmish, Glenda Acland, Nigel Ward, and Barbara Reed, "Describing Records in Context in the Continuum: The Australian Recordkeeping Metadata Schema," *Archivaria* 48 (Fall 1999): 3–37.

use in situations in which such activities may be challenged or audited for their comprehensiveness and accuracy.[8] Creation and ongoing maintenance of such metadata, however, is complex, time consuming, and resource intensive and may only be justifiable when there is a legal mandate or other risk management incentive or when it is envisaged that the content and metadata may be reused or exploited in previously unanticipated ways, such as in digital asset management systems. By contrast, the Dublin Core Metadata Element Set (DCMES) identifies a relatively small, generic set of metadata elements that can be used by any community, expert or nonexpert, to describe and search across a wide variety of information resources on the World Wide Web. Such metadata standards are necessary to ensure that different kinds of descriptive metadata are able to interoperate with one other and with metadata from nonbibliographic systems of the kind that the data management communities and information creators are generating. Relatively lean metadata records such as those created using the DCMES have the advantage of being cheaper to create and maintain, but they may need to be augmented by other types of metadata in order to address the needs of specific user communities and to adequately describe particular types of collection materials.[9]

Another form of metadata that has recently begun to appear is user created; user-created metadata has been gathering momentum in a variety of venues on the Web. Just as many members of the general public have participated in the development of Web content, whether through personal Web pages or by uploading photos onto Flickr or videos onto YouTube, they have also increasingly been getting into the business of creating, sharing, and copying metadata (albeit often unknowingly). Folksonomies that are created using specialized tagging tools in various Web-based communities in order to identify, retrieve, categorize, and promote Web content and the sharing of bookmarks through the practice of social bookmarking are examples of the burgeoning user-created metadata on the Web. Among the advantages of these approaches is that individual Web communities such as affinity groups or hobbyists may be able to create metadata that addresses their specific needs and vocabularies in ways that information professionals who apply metadata standards designed to cater to a wide range of audiences cannot. User-generated metadata is also a comparatively inexpensive way to augment existing metadata, with the cost and the sense of ownership shared among more parties than just those who create information repositories. The disadvantages of user-generated metadata relate to quality control (or lack thereof) and idiosyncrasies

---

[9] See Roy Tennant, "Metadata's Bitter Harvest," *Library Journal*, August 15, 2004, available at http://www.libraryjournal.com/article/CA434443.html; and the Digital Library Federation's Multiple Metadata Formats page at http://webservices.itcs.umich.edu/mediawiki/oaibp/index.php/MultipleMetadataFormats.

that can impede the trustworthiness of both metadata and the resource it describes and negatively affect interoperability between metadata and the resources it is intended to describe. Issues of interoperability are discussed in some detail in the third chapter of this book.

Categorizing Metadata

All these perspectives on metadata should be considered in the development of networked digital information systems, but they lead to a very broad and often confusing conception. To understand this conception better, it is helpful to separate metadata into distinct categories—administrative, descriptive, preservation, use, and technical metadata—that reflect key aspects of metadata functionality. Table 2 defines each of these metadata categories and gives examples of common functions that each might perform in a digital information system.

Table 2. **Different Types of Metadata and Their Functions**

Type	Definition	Examples
Administrative	Metadata used in managing and administering collections and information resources	• Acquisition information • Rights and reproduction tracking • Documentation of legal access requirements • Location information • Selection criteria for digitization
Descriptive	Metadata used to identify and describe collections and related information resources	• Cataloging records • Finding aids • Differentiations between versions • Specialized indexes • Curatorial information • Hyperlinked relationships between resources • Annotations by creators and users
Preservation	Metadata related to the preservation management of collections and information resources	• Documentation of physical condition of resources • Documentation of actions taken to preserve physical and digital versions of resources, e.g., data refreshing and migration • Documentation of any changes occurring during digitization or preservation
Technical	Metadata related to how a system functions or metadata behaves	• Hardware and software documentation • Technical digitization information, e.g., formats, compression ratios, scaling routines • Tracking of system response times • Authentication and security data, e.g., encryption keys, passwords
Use	Metadata related to the level and type of use of collections and information resources	• Circulation records • Physical and digital exhibition records • Use and user tracking • Content reuse and multiversioning information • Search logs • Rights metadata

Table 3. **Attributes and Characteristics of Metadata**

Attribute	Characteristics	Examples
Source of metadata	Internal metadata generated by the creating agent for an information object at the time when it is first created or digitized	• File names and header information • Directory structures • File format and compression scheme
	Metadata intrinsic to an item or work	• A title or other inscription added to an art work by its creator • A title or subtitle on the title page of a manuscript or printed book
	External metadata relating to an original item or information object, that is created later, often by someone other than the original creator	• URLs and other digital statements of provenance • "Tracked changes" • Registrarial and cataloging records • Rights and other legal information
Method of metadata creation	Automatic metadata generated by a computer	• Keyword indexes • User transaction logs • Audit trails
	Manual metadata created by humans	• Descriptive metadata such as catalog records, finding aids, and specialized indexes
Nature of metadata	Nonexpert metadata created by persons who are neither subject specialists nor information professionals, e.g., the original creator of the information object or a folksonomist	• META tags created for a personal Web page • Personal filing systems • Folksonomies
	Expert metadata created by subject specialists and/or information professionals, often not the original creator of the information object	• Specialized subject headings • MARC records • Archival finding aids • Catalog entries for museum objects • Ad hoc metadata created by subject experts, e.g., notations by scholars or researchers
Status	Static metadata that does not or should not change once it has been created	• Technical information such as the date(s) of creation and modification of an information object, how it was created, file size
	Dynamic metadata that may change with use, manipulation, or preservation of an information object	• Directory structure • User transaction logs
	Long-term metadata necessary to ensure that the information object continues to be accessible and usable	• Technical format and processing information • Rights information • Preservation management documentation
	Short-term metadata, mainly of a transactional nature	• Interim location information
Structure	Structured metadata that conforms to a predictable standardized or proprietary structure	• MARC • TEI • EAD • CDWA Lite • Local database formats
	Unstructured metadata that does not conform to a predictable structure	• Unstructured note fields and other free-text annotations

Attribute	Characteristics	Examples
Semantics	Controlled metadata that conforms to a standardized vocabulary or authority form, and that follows standard content (i.e., cataloging) rules	• LCSH, LCNAF, AAT, ULAN, TGM, TGN • AACR (RDA), DACS, CCO
	Uncontrolled metadata that does not conform to any standardized vocabulary or authority form	• Free-text notes • HTML META tags and other user-created tags
Level	Collection-level metadata relating to collections of original items and/or information objects	• Collection- or group-level record, e.g., a MARC record for a group or collection of items; a finding aid for an intact archival collection • Specialized index
	Item-level metadata relating to individual items and/or information objects, often contained within collections	• Catalog records for individual bibliographic items or unique cultural objects • Transcribed image captions and dates • "Tombstone" information for works of art and material culture • Format information

In addition to its different types and functions, metadata exhibits many different characteristics. Table 3 presents some key characteristics of metadata, with examples.

Metadata creation and management have become a complex mix of manual and automatic processes and layers created by many different functions and individuals at different points during the life cycle of an information object. One emergent area is metadata management, the aim of which is to ensure that the metadata we rely on to validate Web resources is itself trustworthy and that the large volume of metadata that potentially can accumulate throughout the life of a Web resource is subject to a summarization and disposition regime.[10]

Figure 1 illustrates the different phases through which information objects typically move during their life cycles in today's digital environment.[11] As they move through each phase in their life cycles, information objects acquire layers of metadata that can be associated with them in several ways. Different types of metadata can become associated with an information object by a variety of processes, both human and

---

[10] See Anne J. Gilliland, Nadav Rouche, Joanne Evans, and Lori Lindberg, "Towards a Twenty-first Century Metadata Infrastructure Supporting the Creation, Preservation and Use of Trustworthy Records: Developing the InterPARES2 Metadata Schema Registry," *Archival Science* 5, no. 1 (March 2005): 43–78.

[11] Modified from Information Life Cycle, *Social Aspects of Digital Libraries: A Report of the UCLA-NSF Social Aspects of Digital Libraries Workshop* (Los Angeles, CA: Graduate School of Education and Information Studies, November 1996), p. 7.

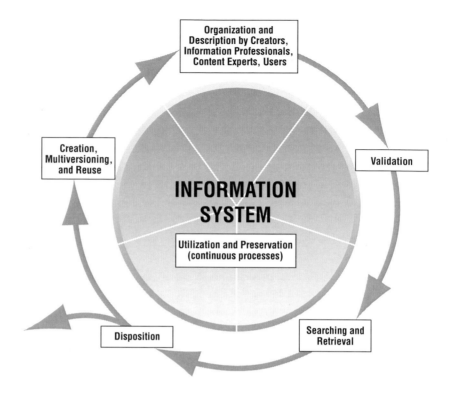

Figure 1. **The Life Cycle of an Information Object**

automated. These layers of accrued metadata can be contained within the same "envelope" as the information object—for example, in the form of header information for an image file or through some form of metadata bundling, for example via METS, which packages structural, descriptive, administrative, and other metadata with an information object or digital surrogate and indicates the types of relationships among the various parts of complex information objects (e.g., a digital surrogate consisting of a series of images representing the pages in a book or in an album of illustrations, or the constituent parts of a decorative arts object such as a tea service). Metadata can also be attached to the information object through bidirectional pointers or hyperlinks, while the relationships between metadata and information objects, and between different aspects of metadata, can be documented by registering them with a metadata registry. However, in any instance in which it is critical that metadata and content coexist, it is highly recommended that the metadata become an integral part of the information object, that is, that it be "embedded" in the object and not stored or linked elsewhere.

As systems designers increasingly respond to the need to incorporate and manage metadata in information systems and to address how to ensure the ongoing viability of both information objects and their associated metadata forward through time, many additional mechanisms for associating metadata with information objects are likely to become available. Metadata registries and schema record-keeping systems are also more likely to develop as it becomes increasingly necessary to document schema evolution and to alert implementers to version changes.[12]

Primary Functions of Metadata

- *Creation, multiversioning, reuse, and recontextualization of information objects.* Objects enter a digital information system by being created digitally or by being converted into digital format. Multiple versions of the same object may be created for preservation, research, exhibit, dissemination, or even product-development purposes. Some administrative and descriptive metadata may and indeed should be included by the creator or digitizer, especially if reuse is envisaged, such as in a digital asset management (DAM) system.
- *Organization and description.* A primary function of metadata is the description and ordering of original objects or items in a repository or collection, as well as of the information objects relating to the originals. Information objects are automatically or manually organized into the structure of the digital information system and may include descriptions generated by the original creator. Additional metadata may be created by information professionals through registration, cataloging, and indexing processes or by others via folksonomies and other forms of user-contributed metadata.
- *Validation.* Users scrutinize metadata and other aspects of retrieved resources in order to ascertain the authoritativeness and trustworthiness of those resources.
- *Searching and retrieval.* Good descriptive metadata is essential to users' ability to find and retrieve relevant metadata and information objects. Locally stored as well as virtually distributed information objects are subject to search and retrieval by users, and information systems create and maintain metadata that tracks retrieval algorithms, user transactions, and system effectiveness in storage and retrieval.

---

[12] See Gilliland et al., "Towards a Twenty-first Century Metadata Infrastructure."

- *Utilization and preservation.* In the digital realm, information objects may be subject to many different kinds of uses
  throughout their lives, during which processes they may also
  be reproduced and modified. Metadata related to user anno-
  tations, rights tracking, and version control may be created.
  Digital objects, especially those that are born digital, also need
  to be subject to a continuous preservation regime and undergo
  processes such as refreshing, migration, and integrity checking
  to ensure their continued availability and to document any
  changes that might have occurred to the information object
  during preservation processes.
- *Disposition.* Metadata is a key component in documenting the
  disposition (e.g., accessioning, deaccessioning) of original objects
  and items in a repository, as well as of the information objects
  relating to those originals. Information objects that are inactive
  or no longer necessary may be discarded.

Some Little-Known Facts about Metadata

- *Metadata does not have to be digital.* Cultural heritage and information professionals have been creating metadata for as long as
  they have been managing collections. Increasingly, such metadata
  is being incorporated into digital information systems, but metadata can also be recorded in analog formats such as card catalogs,
  vertical files, and file labels.
- *Metadata relates to more than the description of an object.* While
  museum, archive, and library professionals may be most familiar
  with the term in association with description or cataloging,
  metadata can also indicate the context, management, processing,
  preservation, and use of the resources being described.
- *Metadata can come from a variety of sources.* Metadata can be
  supplied by a human (by the creator of the digital file, by an
  information professional, and/or by an expert or nonexpert user).
  It can also be generated automatically by a computer algorithm,
  or inferred through a relationship to another resource such as a
  hyperlink.
- *Metadata continues to accrue during the life of an information
  object or system.* Metadata is created, modified, and sometimes
  even disposed of at many points during the life of a resource.
- *One information object's metadata can simultaneously be another
  information object's data, depending on the kinds of aggregations
  of and dependencies between information objects and systems.* The
  distinctions between what constitutes data and what constitutes

metadata can often be very fluid and may depend on how one wishes to use a certain information object.

Why Is Metadata Important?

Metadata consists of complex constructs that can be expensive to create and maintain. How, then, can one justify the cost and effort involved? The development of the World Wide Web and other networked digital information systems has provided information professionals with many opportunities while at the same time requiring them to confront issues that they have not had occasion to explore previously. Judiciously crafted metadata, wherever possible conforming to national and international standards, has become one of the tools that information professionals are using to exploit some of these opportunities, as well as to address some emerging issues, discussed below.

Increased accessibility: Effectiveness of searching can be significantly enhanced through the existence of rich, consistent, carefully crafted descriptive metadata. Metadata can also make it possible to search across multiple collections or to create virtual collections from materials that are distributed across several repositories—but only if the descriptive metadata records are the same or can be mapped across all the collections. (Mary Woodley discusses this in more detail in the third chapter of this book.) Metadata standards that have been developed by different professional communities but include some common data elements (e.g. title, date, creator), such as CDWA Lite, Dublin Core, EAD, MARC XML, MODS, and TEI, are making it easier for users to negotiate between descriptive surrogates of information objects and digital versions of the objects themselves and to search at both the item and collection levels within and across information systems.[13]

Retention of context: Museum, archival, and library repositories do not simply hold objects. They maintain collections of objects that have complex interrelationships among themselves and a variety of associations with people, places, movements or styles, and events. In the digital world it is not unusual for a single object from a collection to be digitized and then for that digital surrogate to become separated from both its own cataloging information (descriptive metadata) and its relationship to the other objects in the same collection, resulting in a decontextualized information object. Metadata plays a crucial role in documenting and maintaining important relationships, as well as in indicating the authenticity, structural and procedural integrity, and degree of completeness of information objects. In an

---

[13] See, e.g., the LEADERS Project, http://www.ucl.ac.uk/leaders-project/index.htm.

archive, for example, by documenting the content, context, and structure of an archival record, metadata in the form of an archival finding aid is what helps to distinguish that record from decontextualized information.

Expanding use: Digital information systems for museum and archival collections make it easier to disseminate digital versions of unique objects to users around the globe who, for reasons of geography, economics, or other barriers, might otherwise not have an opportunity to view them. With new communities of users, however, come new challenges concerning how to make the materials most intellectually accessible. These new communities of users may have significantly different needs, language skills, and information-seeking behaviors from those of the traditional users for whom many existing information services were originally designed.

Learning metadata: Teachers, schoolchildren, and college students may want to search for and use information objects in quite different ways from those of scholarly researchers. Instructors may wish to develop lesson plans, or to scaffold learning so that students build on prior knowledge or are introduced to technical terminology. Specialized forms of metadata have been developed to address these needs.[14]

System development and enhancement: Metadata can document changing uses of systems and content, and that information can in turn feed back into systems development decisions. Well-structured metadata can also facilitate an almost infinite number of ways for users to search for information, to present results, and even to manipulate and to present information objects without compromising their integrity.

Multiversioning: The existence of information about, and surrogates of, cultural objects in digital form has heightened interest in the ability to create multiple and variant versions of information objects. This process may be as simple as creating both a high-resolution copy of a digital image for preservation or scholarly research purposes and a low-resolution thumbnail image that can be rapidly transferred over a network for quick reference purposes. Or it may involve creating variant or derivative forms to be used, for example, in publications, exhibitions, or schoolrooms. In either case, there must be metadata to relate the multiple versions of a given information object and to capture what is the same and what is different about each version. The metadata must also be able to distinguish what is qualitatively different in the various digitized versions or surrogates and the original physical object or item.

Legal issues: Metadata allows repositories to track the many layers of rights, licensing, and reproduction information that exist for original items as well as for their related information objects and the multiple

---

[14] See, e.g., Gateway to Educational Materials, http://www.thegateway.org/about/gemin-general/about-gem/; and IEEE 1484.12.1—2002 Standard for Learning Object Metadata.

versions of those information objects. Metadata also documents other legal or donor requirements that have been imposed on original objects and their surrogates—for example, privacy concerns, restrictions on reproductions, and proprietary and commercial interests. (See "Rights Metadata Made Simple," p. 63.)

Preservation and persistence: If digital information objects that are currently being created are to have a chance of surviving migrations through successive generations of computer hardware and software, or removal to entirely new delivery systems, they will need to have metadata that enables them to exist independently of the system that is currently being used to store and retrieve them. Technical, descriptive, and preservation metadata that documents how a digital information object was created and maintained, how it behaves, and how it relates to other information objects will be essential. It should be noted that for the information objects to remain accessible and intelligible over time, it will also be essential to preserve and migrate this metadata and to ensure that it does not become "disconnected" from the object that it describes.

System improvement and economics: Benchmark technical data, much of which can be collected automatically by a computer, is necessary to evaluate and refine systems in order to make them more effective and efficient from a technical and economic standpoint. The data can also be used in planning for new systems.

A Note on Metadata, Version Control, Reuse, and Recontextualization

It is worth giving special mention to the roles that metadata increasingly needs to play in supporting some of the particular opportunities of the digital age. Historically, one goal of cataloging was to make it possible to distinguish one version of an object or work from another. An item might be different, for example, because it was a second edition of the same work, because it contained distinctive printing anomalies from other copies printed at the same time, because it was an abridged or translated version of the original title, or because its title had changed.[15] Various standardized practices exist to help catalogers alert potential users to such differences in versions of a work. Today metadata must still be able to

---

[15] According to the FRBR conceptual model, these are different "expressions" and/or "manifestations" of a work. See http://www.ifla.org/VII/s13/frbr/frbr.htm. Note that the definition of a "work" (and the conceptual model) can differ considerably for unique works of art or architecture, as opposed to literary works or musical compositions, for which the FRBR model is ideal. See Murtha Baca and Sherman Clarke, "FRBR and Works of Art, Architecture, and Material Culture," in *Understanding FRBR: What It Is and How It Will Affect Our Retrieval Tools*, ed. Arlene G. Taylor (Westport, CT: Libraries Unlimited, 2007), pp. 103–10.

elucidate such distinctions. However, it must also be able to help users distinguish between, and trace the changes in, the following:

- Original analog and digitized versions, noting any changes that might have occurred accidentally or deliberately during the digitization process (e.g., digital "repair" of a broken glass lantern slide).
- Digitized and born digital objects that are created in a range of resolutions to facilitate a variety of distribution mechanisms and uses, or that are periodically refreshed or migrated or rendered into an alternate format for preservation and long-term storage or security purposes.
- Original and renamed or retitled or reattributed objects. For example, museum objects may be renamed or reattributed or assigned a different creation date because new documentation has come to light. Metadata may also change due to cultural sensitivities or provenancial challenges; for example, place-names or object names may be changed to their original Native American forms, with English-language names assigned after the objects' creation "demoted" to the status of variants or additional access points.
- Original born digital materials and revised or updated versions (e.g., Web pages, reference databases).
- Original analog or born digital materials that are reused in part or in whole in new digital resources (e.g., personal Web pages, digital art, or digital music compilations).
- Objects, especially but not only museum objects, that are described collectively in one context within their metadata (e.g., as objects that were all collected at the same time at the same archaeological excavation) but are then taken individually out of that collection and recontextualized (e.g., in a special exhibition of Greek vases from a particular period or an exhibition of paintings relating to a particular theme or subject).

Conclusion and Outstanding Questions

Metadata is like interest: it accrues over time. To stretch the metaphor further, wise investments generate the best return on intellectual capital. Carefully crafted metadata results in the best information management—and the best end-user access—in both the short and the long term. If thorough, consistent metadata has been created, it is possible to conceive of it being used in an almost infinite number of new and even currently unforeseen ways to meet the needs of both traditional and nontraditional users, for multiversioning, and for data mapping and mining. But the resources and intellectual and technical design issues involved in good metadata development and management are far from trivial. Some key questions that must be resolved by information professionals as they develop digital information systems and objects are:

- identifying which metadata schema or schemas should be applied in order to best meet the needs of the information creator, repository, and users. As mentioned above, selection of an inappropriate schema (e.g., EAD for museum collections that do not share a common provenance) serves neither the collection materials themselves nor the users who wish to find, understand, and use those materials. Also, in many cases, especially with complex objects or hierarchically structured archival and other types of collections, a combination of schemas working together (e.g., MARC and/or EAD at the collection level; MARC, Dublin Core, MODS, VRA Core, or CDWA Lite at the item level) may be the best solution.

- deciding which aspects of metadata are essential for the desired goal and how granular each type of metadata needs to be—in other words, how much is enough and how much is too much. There will likely always be important tradeoffs between the costs of developing and managing metadata to meet current needs and creating sufficient metadata that can be capitalized on for future, often unanticipated uses. Metadata creators should remember that good "core" metadata can be a valid approach both in economic and in intellectual terms; see Principles 2 and 7 of "Practical Principles for Metadata Creation and Maintenance," pp. 71-72.

- ensuring that the metadata schemas and controlled vocabularies, thesauri, and taxonomies (including folksonomies) being applied are the most up-to-date, complete versions of those sets of data values and that they are the appropriate terminologies for the materials being described and for the intended users.

What we do know is that the existence of many types of metadata will prove critical to the continued online and intellectual accessibility and utility of digital resources and the information objects that they contain, as well as the original objects and collections to which they relate. In this sense, metadata provides us with the Rosetta stone that will make it possible to decode information objects and their transformation into knowledge in the cultural heritage information systems of the future.

Metadata and the Web

Tony Gill

When the first edition of this book was published in 1998, the term *metadata* was comparatively esoteric, having originated in the information science and geospatial data communities before being co-opted and partially redefined by the library, archive, and museum information communities at the end of the twentieth century. Today, nearly a decade later, a Google search on "metadata" yields about 58 million results (see Web Search Engines sidebar). Metadata has quietly hit the big time; it is now a consumer commodity. For example, almost all consumer-level digital cameras capture and embed Exchangeable Image File Format (EXIF)[1] metadata in digital images, and files created using Adobe's Creative Suite of software tools (e.g. Photoshop) contain embedded Extensible Metadata Platform (XMP)[2] metadata.

As the term *metadata* has been increasingly adopted and co-opted by more diverse audiences, the definition of what constitutes metadata has grown in scope to include almost anything that describes anything else. The standard concise definition of metadata is "data about data," a relationship that is frequently illustrated using the metaphor of a library card catalog. The first few lines of the following Wikipedia entry for *metadata* are typical:

> **Metadata** (Greek: meta- + Latin: data "information"), literally "data about data," are information about another set of data. A common example is a library catalog card, which contains data about the contents and location of a book: They are data about the data in the book referred to by the card.[3]

The library catalog card metaphor is pedagogically useful because it is nonthreatening. Most people are familiar with the concept of a card catalog as a simple tool to help readers find the books they are looking for and to help librarians manage a library's collection as a whole. However, the example is problematic from an ontological perspective, because

---

[1] See http://www.exif.org/.

[2] See http://www.adobe.com/products/xmp/.

neither catalog cards nor books are, in fact, data. They are *containers* or *carriers* of data. This distinction between information and its carrier is increasingly being recognized; for example, the CIDOC Conceptual Reference Model (CRM),[4] a domain ontology for the semantic interchange of museum, library, and archive information, models the relationship between information objects—identifiable conceptual entities such as a text, an image, an algorithm, or a musical composition—and their physical carrier as follows:

> E73 Information Object *P128 is carried by* E24 Physical Man-Made Stuff

The IFLA Functional Requirements for Bibliographic Records (FRBR)[5] model makes a similar four-tier distinction between Works, Representations, Manifestations, and Items: the first three entities are conceptual entities, and only Items are actual physical instances represented by bibliographic entities.

Of course, most library catalogs are now stored as *0*s and *1*s in computer databases, and the "items" representing the "works" that they

---

Web Search Engines

Web search engines such as Google are automated information retrieval systems that continuously traverse the Web, visiting Web sites and saving copies of the pages and their locations as they go in order to build up a huge catalog of fully indexed Web pages. They typically provide simple yet powerful keyword searching facilities and extremely large result sets that are relevance ranked using closely guarded proprietary algorithms in an effort to provide the most useful results. The most well known Web search engines are available at no cost to the end-user and are primarily supported by advertising revenue. Web search engines rely heavily on Title HTML tags (a simple but very important type of metadata that appears in the title bar and favorites/bookmarks menus of most browsers), the actual words on the Web page (unstructured data), and referring links (indicating the popularity of the Web resource).

---

[3] http://en.wikipedia.org/wiki/Metadata.

[4] Nick Crofts, Martin Doerr, Tony Gill, Stephen Stead, and Matthew Stiff, eds., *Definition of the CIDOC Conceptual Reference Model*, version 4.2, June 2005. Available at http://cidoc.ics.forth.gr/docs/cidoc_crm_version_4.2.1.pdf. See also Tony Gill, "Building Semantic Bridges between Museums, Libraries and Archives: The CIDOC Conceptual Reference Model," *First Monday* 9, no. 5 (May 3, 2004). Available at http://www.firstmonday.org/issues/issue9_5/gill/index.html.

[5] *Functional Requirements for Bibliographic Records* (IFLA, 1998). http://www.ifla.org/VII/s13/frbr/frbr.htm.

describe (to use the nomenclature of the FRBR model) are increasingly likely to be digital objects on a Web server, as opposed to ink, paper, and cardboard objects on shelves (this is even more true now in light of large-scale bibliographic digitization initiatives such as the Google Book Search Library Project, the Million Books Project, and the Open Content Alliance, about which more later).

So if we use the term *metadata* in a strict sense, to refer only to *data about data*, we end up in the strange predicament whereby a record in a library catalog can be called metadata if it describes an electronic resource but cannot be called metadata if it describes a physical object such as a book. This is clearly preposterous and illustrates the shortcomings of the standard concise definition.

Another property of metadata that is not addressed adequately by the standard concise definition is that metadata is normally structured to model the most important attributes of the type of object that it describes. Returning to the library catalog example, each component of a standard MARC bibliographic record is clearly delineated by field labels that identify the meaning of each atomic piece of information, for example, author, title, subject.

The structured nature of metadata is important. By accurately modeling the most essential attributes of the class of information objects being described, metadata in aggregate can serve as a catalog—a distillation of the essential attributes of the collection of information objects—thereby becoming a useful tool for using and managing that collection. In the context of this chapter, then, *metadata* can be defined as *a structured description of the essential attributes of an information object.*

The Web Continues to Grow

The World Wide Web is the largest collection of documents the world has ever seen, and its growth is showing no signs of slowing. Although it is impossible to determine the exact size of the Web, some informative metrics are available. The July 2007 Netcraft survey of Web hosts received responses to HTTP (HyperText Transfer Protocol, the data transmission language of the Web) requests for server names from 125,626,329 "sites."[6] A site in this case represents a unique hostname such as http://www.host name.com. The same survey in January 1996 received responses from just 77,128 Web servers; the number of Web servers connected to the Internet has grown exponentially over the past decade or so. (Fig. 1.)

---

[6] *Netcraft Web Server Survey*, July 2007. http://news.netcraft.com/archives/2007/07/09/july_2007_web_server_survey.html.

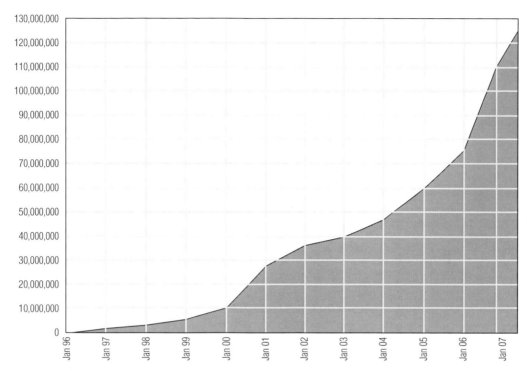

Figure 1. **Growth in the Number of Web Hosts, January 1996–July 2007.** (Source: Netcraft Survey. http://www.netcraft.com/survey/)

Although the Netcraft Web hosts survey clearly demonstrates the continuing upward trend in the growth of the Web, it does not tell the whole story because it does not address how many Web sites are hosted on each server or how many accessible pages are contained in each site.

The Visible Web versus the Hidden Web

Accurate figures for the number of pages available on the Web are much more difficult to find; two computer scientists estimated that the indexable Web comprised more than 11.5 billion pages at the end of January 2005,[7] although given the rapid increase in the amount of information on the Web, that figure is now hopelessly out of date.

The problem of determining how many pages are available on the Web is exacerbated by the fact that a large and increasing amount of the Web's content is served dynamically from databases in response to a user's input, or is in a non-Web format, or requires some kind of user authentica-

---

[7] Antonio Gulli and Alessio Signorini, "The Indexable Web Is More than 11.5 Billion Pages." http://www.cs.uiowa.edu/~asignori/web-size/.

tion or login. Web crawlers, also called spiders or robots (the software used by search engines to trawl the Web for content and build their vast indices), can only index the so-called Visible Web; they cannot submit queries to databases, parse file formats that they do not recognize, click buttons on Web forms, or log in to sites requiring authentication, so all of this content is effectively invisible to the search engines and is not indexed.

Collectively, this content beyond the reach of search engine Web crawlers is referred to as the Deep Web, the Invisible Web, or the Hidden Web, and as these names suggest, estimating its size is even more difficult than measuring the public or Visible Web. A survey published in 2001 claimed that the Deep Web was five hundred times larger than the Visible/Indexable Web,[8] although very little meaningful information can be inferred from this today; in terms of the evolution of the Internet, five years is the equivalent of a geologic era.

Although much of the content on the Deep Web is deliberately kept out of the public sphere, either because it is private or because some kind of fee or subscription must be paid to access it, there is a vast amount of information that is inadvertently inaccessible to Web search engines simply because it is contained in Web sites that were not designed to be accessible to the search engines' Web crawlers. This is an especially common problem for sites that generate pages dynamically in response to user input using content stored in databases. Because Web search engines often account for the vast majority of a Web site's traffic, building sites that are not accessible to Web crawlers can seriously limit the accessibility and use of the information they contain. Institutions seeking to make dynamically generated information as widely accessible as possible should design "crawler-friendly" Web sites. A good way to do this, which also facilitates access by human users (as opposed to Web robots), is to provide access to information through hyperlinked hierarchies of categories, in addition to search interfaces. Another option for the museum, library, and archive sectors is to contribute otherwise Deep Web collections information to union catalogs or other aggregated resources that are indexed by the commercial search engines.

Search engine providers are now also providing tools to help Webmasters expose otherwise hidden content; for example, Google's Sitemap feature allows Webmasters to provide a detailed list of all the pages on their sites—even those that are dynamically generated—in a variety of machine-readable formats to ensure that every page gets crawled and indexed correctly. (Both union catalogs and tools to expose Deep Web content to search engines are discussed in more detail later in this chapter.)

---

[8] Michael K. Bergman, "The Deep Web: Surfacing Hidden Value," *Journal of Electronic Publishing* 7, no. 1 (August 2001). http://www.press.umich.edu/jep/07-01/bergman.html.

Finding Needles in a Huge and Rapidly Expanding Haystack

The Web is the largest and fastest-growing collection of documents the world has ever seen, and it has undoubtedly revolutionized access to an unimaginable amount of information, of widely variable quality, for the estimated 1 billion people who now have access to it[9]—although it is worth remembering that this is still less than one person in six globally (the myth of nearly universal access to the Web remains just that—a myth).

Unfortunately, however, finding relevant, high-quality information on the Web is not always a straightforward proposition. There is no overarching logical structure to the Web, and the core Web protocols do not offer any support for information search and retrieval beyond the basic mechanisms provided by the HTTP for requesting and retrieving pages from a specific Web address.

The disappointment of the hypertext community with the World Wide Web is clearly evident in a comment by Ted Nelson (who first coined the term *hypertext* in 1965) in a speech delivered at the HyperText 97 conference: "The reaction of the hypertext research community to the World Wide Web is like finding out that you have a fully grown child. And it's a delinquent."[10]

Not surprisingly, tools designed to address the resource location problem and help make sense of the Web's vast information resources started to appear soon after the launch of the first Web browsers in the early 1990s; for example, Tim Berners-Lee founded the WWW Virtual Library,[11] a distributed directory of Web sites maintained by human editors, shortly after inventing the Web itself, and search engines such as Yahoo![12] Lycos,[13] and Webcrawler[14] were launched in 1994.

The clear market leader in Web search today is Google. According to a Nielsen//NetRatings press release issued on March 30, 2006, "Google accounts for nearly half of all Web searches, while approximately one-third are conducted on Yahoo! and MSN combined."[15] According to its Web

---

[9] "Worldwide Internet Users Top 1 Billion in 2005," Computer Industry Almanac Inc., January 4, 2006. http://www.c-i-a.com/pr0106.htm.

[10] Ted Nelson, speaking at HyperText 97, Eighth ACM International Hypertext Conference, Southampton, April 6–11, 1997. Quoted in Nick Gibbins, "The Eighth ACM International Hypertext Conference," Ariadne, no. 9 (May 1997). http://www.ariadne.ac.uk/issue9/hypertext/.

[11] WWW Virtual Library: http://vlib.org/.

[12] http://www.yahoo.com/.

[13] http://www.lycos.com/.

[14] http://www.Webcrawler.com/.

[15] Press Release: "Google Accounts for Nearly Half of All Web Searches, While Approximately One-Third Are Conducted on Yahoo! and MSN Combined, According to Nielsen//Netratings, Nielson//NetRatings," March 30, 2006. http://www.nielsen-netratings.com/pr/pr_060330.pdf.

site, "Google's mission is to organize the world's information and make it universally accessible and useful."[16] In the relatively short time since the company's launch in 1998 in a garage in Menlo Park, California, it has grown to become one of the Internet's giants: it employs almost six thousand people, operates one of the five most popular Web sites on the Internet, and has a current market valuation of over $115 billion, making it the second-largest technology company in the world after Microsoft. Helping people find information on the Web is big business.

To maintain its position as the most popular search engine on the Web, Google must routinely perform several Herculean tasks that are becoming increasingly difficult as both the Web and the number of people using it continue to grow. First, it must maintain an index of the public Web that is both sufficiently current and sufficiently comprehensive to remain competitive. Currency is important because, as the Google Zeitgeist demonstrates,[17] many of the most popular searches are related to current affairs and popular culture. Any search engine that fails to maintain a sufficiently current index will not be able to deliver relevant results to queries about current events and will rapidly lose a large share of the global search market.

Second, a search engine must have an adequately comprehensive index of the Web, because otherwise it may fail to deliver relevant results that a competitor with a more comprehensive index could provide. A study by Gulli and Signorini estimated that as of January 2005 Google had indexed about 76 percent of the 11.5 billion pages on the Visible Web.[18] Index size has traditionally been one of the key metrics on which search engines compete, so in August 2005 Yahoo! issued a press release claiming to have indexed 19 billion Web pages.[19] If the Gulli and Signorini estimate of the size of the Web is to be believed, the Yahoo! claim would imply that the Web had doubled in size in just seven months, and consequently some commentators have conducted further research, which casts doubt on the veracity of the Yahoo! figures.[20]

Third, in addition to maintaining a current and comprehensive index of the rapidly expanding Web, a search engine must be able to search the index that it has compiled by crawling the Web, ranking the search results according to relevance, and presenting the results to the user as quickly as possible—ideally in less than half a second. Much of Google's

---

[16] Google Company Overview: http://www.google.com/corporate/index.html.

[17] Google Zeitgeist: http://www.google.com/press/zeitgeist.html.

[18] Gulli and Signorini, "The Indexable Web Is More than 11.5 Billion Pages."

[19] Tim Mayer, "Our Blog Is Growing Up—And So Has Our Index," Yahoo! Search Blog, August 8, 2005. http://www.ysearchblog.com/archives/000172.html.

[20] Matthew Cheney and Mike Perry, "A Comparison of the Size of the Yahoo! and Google Indices, 2005." http://vburton.ncsa.uiuc.edu/oldstudy.html.

rapid rise to dominance in the search engine market can be attributed to its sophisticated and patented PageRank™ relevance ranking algorithm, which ranks the importance of relevant pages according to the number of links from other pages that point to them.[21] The PageRank™ value of each Web page and the text contained in the Title HTML tag are really the only metadata that Google uses to any meaningful extent in providing its search service—the search itself is performed on an index of the actual data content of the HTML pages. Fourth, a market-leading search engine such as Google must be able to respond to hundreds of millions of such search requests from users all around the world every day.[22]

To meet these gargantuan and constantly increasing information retrieval challenges, Google has developed one of the largest and most powerful computer infrastructures on the planet. Unlike most of its competitors, which typically use small clusters of very powerful servers, Google has developed a massive parallel architecture comprising large numbers of inexpensive networked PCs, which Google claims is both more powerful and more scalable than the use of a smaller number of more powerful servers.[23]

Google's server cluster was reported to comprise more than fifteen thousand PCs in 2003; the company has provided little official information about its hardware recently, but given the explosive growth in both the amount of information on the Web and the number of Web users, coupled with a wide range of new services offered by Google (e.g., Google Print, Google Scholar, Google Images, GMail, Froogle, Blogger, Google Earth), the number of server nodes is undoubtedly much greater today. There is widespread speculation on the Web that the Google server cluster today comprises anywhere between 100,000 and 1,000,000 nodes[24] and that it could in fact be the most powerful "virtual supercomputer" in the world.

Can the Search Engines Keep Up?

Can the search engines continue to scale up their operations as both the amount of content on the Web and the number of users continue to grow? This is a difficult question to answer; analysts have been predicting since

---

[21] "Our Search: Google Technology." http://www.google.com/technology/.

[22] Danny Sullivan, "Searches per Day," from SearchEngineWatch.com. http://searchengine-watch.com/reports/article.php/2156461.

[23] Luiz André Barroso, Jeffrey Dean, and Urs Hölzle, "Web Search for a Planet: The Google Cluster Architecture," *IEEE Micro* 23, no. 2 (April 2003). http://labs.google.com/papers/googlecluster-ieee.pdf.

[24] Brian Despain, "*Google—The Network?*" entry for September 22, 2005, on the blog *Thinking Monkey*. http://www.thinkingmonkey.com/2005/09/google-network.shtml.

before the new millennium that the Web would outgrow the search engines' abilities to index it, but so far the tipping point has not been reached.

Steve Lawrence and C. Lee Giles of the NEC Research Center conducted a scientifically rigorous survey of the main search engines' coverage of Web content in February 1999. Their findings, published in the peer-reviewed journal *Nature*, indicated that at that time no search engine indexed more than about 16 percent of the Web: "Our results show that the search engines are increasingly falling behind in their efforts to index the Web."[25] However, compare this with the January 2005 study by Gulli and Signorini,[26] which estimated that Google had indexed about 76 percent of the 11.5 billion pages on the Web, and it seems that the search engines provide significantly better coverage now than they did in the Web's infancy. Clearly, the search engines in general and Google in particular have been able to scale up their technology better than most people predicted at the end of the twentieth century.

But common sense suggests that there has to be some kind of limit to this continuous and rapid expansion. Even if Google's innovative, massively networked supercomputer architecture is technically capable of indefinite expansion, perhaps other kinds of constraints will prove insurmountable at some point in the future. A recent article by one of Google's principal hardware engineers warns that unless the ratio of computer performance to electrical power consumption improves dramatically, power costs may become a larger component of the total cost of ownership (TCO) than initial hardware costs.[27] This could become a significant barrier to the continued expansion of the Google platform in the future, particularly if energy costs continue to rise. A million interconnected servers consume a tremendous amount of electrical power.

Metadata to the Rescue?

In the early days of the Web, many people, particularly in the emerging digital library community, saw metadata as the long-term solution to the problem of resource discovery on the Web. The reasoning behind this was very logical and goes back to the classical example of metadata: Library catalogs had proved their efficacy in providing both access to and control of large bibliographic collections, so why should the Web be different?

Research and development projects to catalog useful Web resources sprang up around the globe, such as the subject gateways funded

---

[25] Steve Lawrence and C. Lee Giles, summary of "Accessibility of Information on the Web," *Nature* 400 (July 9, 1999): 107–9.

[26] Gulli and Signorini, "The Indexable Web Is More than 11.5 Billion Pages."

[27] Luiz André Barroso, "The Price of Performance: An Economic Case for Chip Multi-processing," *ACM Queue* 3, no. 7 (September 2005). http://acmqueue.com/modules. php?=name=Content&pa=showpage&pid=330.

by the Electronic Libraries Programme for the higher education sector in the United Kingdom.[28] One of the first lessons learned from these early pilot projects was that the economics of cataloging Web resources was very different from the economics of cataloging books. Whereas the creation of a carefully crafted (and expensive) MARC record, complete with subject headings and controlled terminology and conforming to standardized cataloging rules, could be justified in the traditional bibliographic world because the record would be used by many different libraries for many years, Web resources are both more dynamic and more transient; unlike books, Web sites often change, and sometimes they disappear altogether.

As a result, metadata standards for describing Internet resources have appeared, such as META tags, the Dublin Core Metadata Element Set (DCMES), and the Resource Description Framework (RDF). These are discussed in more detail below (note, however, that many search engines make little or inconsistent use of embedded metadata, since it cannot always be trusted).

META Tags

The AltaVista search engine originally popularized the use of two simple metadata elements, "keywords" and "description," that can be easily and invisibly embedded in the <HEAD> section of Web pages by their authors using the HTML META tag. Here is an example:

> <META NAME="KEYWORDS" CONTENT="data standards, metadata, Web resources, World Wide Web, cultural heritage information, digital resources, Dublin Core, RDF, Semantic Web">
>
> <META NAME="DESCRIPTION" CONTENT="Version 3.0 of the site devoted to metadata: what it is, its types and uses, and how it can improve access to Web resources; includes a crosswalk.">

The original intention was that the "keyword" metadata could be used to provide more effective retrieval and relevance ranking, whereas the "description" tag would be used in the display of search results to provide an accurate, authoritative summary of the particular Web resource.

Dublin Core

The Dublin Core Metadata Element Set (DCMES)[29] is a set of fifteen information elements that can be used to describe a wide variety of

---

[28] See http://www.ukoln.ac.uk/services/elib/.

[29] *Dublin Core Metadata Element Set, Version 1.1, Reference Description.* http://www.dublincore.org/documents/dces.

resources for the purpose of simple cross-disciplinary resource discovery. Although originally intended solely as the equivalent of a quick and simple "catalog card" for networked resources, the scope of the Dublin Core gradually expanded over the past decade to encompass the description of almost anything. The fifteen elements are *Contributor, Coverage, Creator, Date, Description, Format, Identifier, Language, Publisher, Relation, Rights, Source, Subject, Title*, and *Type*.

The fifteen Dublin Core elements and their meanings have been developed and refined by an international group of librarians, information professionals, and subject specialists through an ongoing consensus-building process that has included more than a dozen international workshops to date, various working groups, and several active electronic mailing lists. The element set has been published as both a national and an international standard (NISO Z39.85-2001 and ISO 15836-2003, respectively). There are now a significant number of large-scale deployments of Dublin Core metadata around the globe.[30]

Resource Description Framework

The Resource Description Framework (RDF)[31] is a standard developed by the World Wide Web Consortium (W3C) for encoding resource descriptions (i.e., metadata) in a way that computers can "understand," share, and process in useful ways. RDF metadata is normally encoded using XML, the Extensible Markup Language.[32] However, as the name suggests, RDF only provides a *framework* for resource description; it provides the formal *syntax*, or structure, component of the resource description language but not the semantic component. The *semantics*, or meaning, must also be specified for a particular application or community in order for computers to be able to make sense of the metadata. The semantics are specified by an RDF vocabulary, which is a knowledge representation or model of the metadata that unambiguously identifies what each individual metadata element means and how it relates to the other metadata elements in the domain. RDF vocabularies can be expressed either as RDF schemas[33] or as more expressive Web Ontology Language (OWL)[34] ontologies.

The CIDOC CRM[35] is a pertinent example of an ontology that provides the semantics for a specific application domain—the interchange of rich museum, library, and archive collection documentation. By expressing the classes and properties of the CIDOC CRM as an RDF

---

[30] *Dublin Core Projects*. http://www.dublincore.org/projects/.

[31] *Resource Description Framework*. http://www.w3.org/RDF/.

[32] *Extensible Markup Language (XML)*. http://www.w3.org/XML/.

[33] *RDF Vocabulary Description Language 1.0: RDF Schema*. http://www.w3.org/TR/rdf-schema/.

[34] OWL Web Ontology Language Guide: http://www.w3.org/TR/owl-guide/.

[35] See http://cidoc.ics.forth.gr/official_release_cidoc.html; and note 4.

schema or OWL ontology, information about cultural heritage collections can be expressed in RDF in a semantically unambiguous way, thereby facilitating information interchange of cultural heritage information across different computer systems.

Using the highly extensible and robust logical framework of RDF, RDF schemas, and OWL, rich metadata descriptions of networked resources can be created that draw on a theoretically unlimited set of semantic vocabularies. Interoperability for automated processing is maintained, however, because the strict underlying XML syntax requires that each vocabulary be explicitly specified.

RDF, RDF schemas, and OWL are all fundamental building blocks of the W3C's Semantic Web[36] activity. The Semantic Web is the vision of Sir Tim Berners-Lee, director of the W3C and inventor of the original World Wide Web: Berners-Lee's vision is for the Web to evolve into a seamless network of interoperable data that can be shared and reused across software, enterprise, and community boundaries.

A Bountiful Harvest

The Open Archives Initiative Protocol for Metadata Harvesting (OAI-PMH)[37] provides an alternative method for making Deep Web metadata more accessible. Rather than embed metadata in the actual content of Web pages, the OAI-PMH is a set of simple protocols that allows metadata records to be exposed on the Web in a predictable way so that other OAI-PMH-compatible computer systems can access and retrieve them. (Fig. 2.)

The OAI-PMH supports interoperability (which can be thought of as the ability of two systems to communicate meaningfully) between two different computer systems; an OAI data provider and an OAI harvester, which in most cases is also an OAI service provider (see Glossary). As the names suggest, an OAI data provider is a source of metadata records, whereas the OAI harvester retrieves (or "harvests") metadata records from one or more OAI data providers. Since both an OAI data provider and an OAI data harvester must conform to the same basic information exchange protocols, metadata records can be reliably retrieved from the provider(s) by the harvester.

Although the OAI-PMH can support any metadata schema that can be expressed in XML, it mandates that all OAI Data Providers must be able to deliver Dublin Core XML metadata records as a minimum requirement. In this way, the OAI-PMH supports *interoperability* of metadata between different systems.

---

[36] Semantic Web. http://www.w3.org/2001/sw/.

[37] Open Archives Initiative: http://www.openarchives.org/.

Google's Sitemap, part of a suite of Webmaster tools offered by that search engine, also supports the OAI-PMH. By exposing a metadata catalog as an OAI data provider and registering it with Google's Sitemap, otherwise Deep Web content can be made accessible to Google's Web crawler, indexed, and made available to the search engine's users.

Meta-Utopia or Metagarbage?

In his oft-quoted diatribe, "Metacrap: Putting the Torch to the Seven Straw-men of the Meta-Utopia,"[38] journalist, blogger, and science fiction writer Cory Doctorow enumerates what he describes as the "seven insurmountable obstacles between the world as we know it and meta-utopia." In this piece, Doctorow, a great proponent of making digital content as widely available as possible, puts forth his arguments for the thesis that metadata created by humans will never have widespread utility as an aid to resource discovery on the Web. These arguments are paraphrased below.

- *"People lie."* Metadata on the Web cannot be trusted, because there are many unscrupulous Web content creators that publish misleading or dishonest metadata in order to draw additional traffic to their sites.
- *"People are lazy."* Most Web content publishers are not sufficiently motivated to do the labor involved in carefully cataloging the content that they publish.
- *"People are stupid."* Most Web content publishers are not smart enough to catalog effectively the content that they publish.
- *"Mission: Impossible—know thyself."* Metadata on the Web cannot be trusted, because there are many Web content creators who inadvertently publish misleading metadata.
- *"Schemas aren't neutral."*[39] Classification schemes are subjective.
- *"Metrics influence results."* Competing metadata standards bodies will never agree.
- *"There's more than one way to describe something."* Resource description is subjective.

Although obviously intended as a satirical piece, Doctorow's short essay nevertheless contains several grains of truth when considering the Web as a whole.

---

[38] Cory Doctorow, "Metacrap: Putting the Torch to the Seven Straw-men of the Meta-Utopia," August 26, 2001. http://www.well.com/~doctorow/metacrap.htm.

[39] Doctorow confusingly uses "schema" here to refer to classification schemes, not the more common meaning of a metadata schema or data structure.

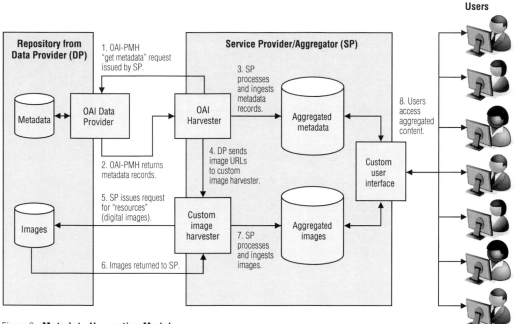

Figure 2. **Metadata Harvesting Model**

Doctorow's most compelling argument is the first one: people lie. It is very easy for unscrupulous Web publishers to embed "META tag spam"—deliberately misleading or dishonest descriptive metadata—in their Web pages. META tag spam is designed to increase the likelihood that a Web site will appear in a search engine's search results and to improve the site's ranking in those results. There is plenty of incentive to increase a Web site's visibility and ranking with the search engines. Increased visibility and higher ranking can dramatically increase the amount of user traffic to a Web site, which results in greater profits for a commercial site's owners and greater success for nonprofit organizations seeking to reach a broader audience. However, the search engine companies have long been wise to this practice, and as a result they either treat embedded metadata with skepticism or ignore it altogether. It is rumored that some search engines may even penalize sites that contain suspect metadata by artificially lowering their page ranking. But because most search engines do not utilize embedded metadata, there is usually no incentive for the vast majority of honest Web publishers to expend the additional time and effort required to add this potentially useful information to their own pages, unless the particular search engine that they use to index their own site makes use of the embedded Keyword and Description META tags originally developed by AltaVista.

Doctorow's other points are less convincing, particularly if we look at the subset of Web content created by museums, libraries, and archives. Librarians, museum documentation staff, and archivists are typically diligent, well-trained information professionals, and they are not usually dishonest, lazy, or stupid. They have a long tradition of using standard metadata element sets (such as MARC, EAD, CDWA Lite, and VRA Core), classification schemes, controlled vocabularies, and community-specific cataloging rules (such as AACR, DACS, and CCO) to describe resources in standardized ways that have been developed over decades of collaborative consensus-building efforts. In effect, they have been demonstrating the value of descriptive metadata created by human beings for centuries.

Playing Tag

Another recent development in the field of metadata on the Web that significantly weakens Doctorow's case are the so-called folksonomies. A folksonomy is developed collaboratively within a specific user community when many people use a shared system to label Web content, such as Web pages or online images, with descriptive terms, or tags. People are individually motivated to tag Web content because it allows them to organize and find the content at a later date; they are effectively building their own personal catalogs of Web content. With folksonomies, any terms or names can be used, without restriction—unlike taxonomic classifications, in which a fixed hierarchical list of carefully constructed descriptive terms must be used.

The folksonomy aspect comes into play when all the tags applied to a specific Web resource by multiple users are aggregated and ranked. If one person applied the term *impressionism* to a Web site, it doesn't really say very much. However, if several hundred people use this term and it is the most commonly used tag for that Web site, then it is a pretty safe bet that the Web site is about Impressionism and Impressionist art.

This is analogous to Google's PageRank™ algorithm: each time an individual user labels a Web resource with a specific descriptive tag, it counts as a "vote" for the appropriateness of that term for describing the resource. In this way, Web resources are effectively cataloged by individuals for their own benefit, but the community also benefits from the additional metadata that is statistically weighted to minimize the effects of either dishonesty or stupidity.

The two most well known examples of folksonomy/tagging sites on the Web are del.icio.us[40] and Flickr.[41] Del.icio.us enables users to create

---

[40] http://del.icio.us.
[41] http://flickr.com/.

tagged personal catalogs of their favorite Internet bookmarks, whereas Flickr is a digital photo sharing site that enables users to tag photos for easier retrieval. It is interesting to note that both companies were acquired by Yahoo! in 2005. Clearly, the world's second most popular search engine company sees significant value in community-generated metadata.

In Metadata We Trust (Sometimes)

Metadata is not a universal panacea for resource discovery on the Web. The underlying issues of trust, authenticity, and authority continue to impede the widespread deployment and use of metadata for Web resource discovery, and this situation is unlikely to change as long as the search engines can continue to satisfy the search needs of most users with their current methods (indexing the Title HTML tags, the actual words on Web pages, and ranking the "popularity" of pages based on the number of referring links).

However, human-created metadata still has an extremely important role within specific communities and applications, especially in the

---

Libraries and the Web

The Web has dramatically changed the global information landscape—a fact that is felt particularly keenly by libraries, the traditional gateways to information for the previous two millennia or so. Whereas previous generations of scholars relied almost entirely on libraries for their research needs, the current generation of students, and even of more advanced scholars, is much more likely to start (and often end) their research with a Web search.

Faced with this new reality, libraries and related service organizations have been working hard to bring information from their online public access catalogs (OPACS), traditionally resources hidden in the Deep Web beyond the reach of the search engines' Web crawlers, out into the open. For example, OCLC has collaborated with Google, Yahoo! and Amazon.com to make an abbreviated version of its WorldCat union catalog acces-

sible as Open WorldCat. The full WorldCat catalog is available only by subscription.

But the most striking example of collaboration between libraries and a search engine company to date is undoubtedly the Google Book Search–Library Project.[1] This massive initiative, announced late in 2004, aims to make the full text of the holdings of five leading research libraries—Harvard University Library, the University of Michigan Library, the New York Public Library, Oxford University Library, and Stanford University Library—searchable on the Visible Web via Google.

By adding the full text of millions of printed volumes to its search index, the Google Book Search–Library Project will enable users to search for words in the text of the books themselves. However, the results of searches will depend on the works' copyright status. For a book that is in the public domain, Google will provide a brief bibliographic record, links to buy it online, and the full text. For a book that is still in copyright, however, Google will provide only a brief bibliographic record, small excerpts of the text in which the search term appears (the size of the excerpts depends on whether the copyright holder is a participant in the Google Books Partner Program,[2] a companion program for publishers), and links to various online booksellers where it can be purchased.

It is perhaps ironic that, due to the dysfunctional and anachronistic state of existing copyright legislation, this scenario is almost the exact reverse of the familiar library catalog metadata example: Rather than search metadata catalogs in order to gain access to full online texts, the Google model helps users to search full online texts in order to find metadata records!

But open access to the rich content of printed books is clearly an idea whose time has come. The Google Book Search–Library Project may be the most ambitious project of its kind to date, but it is neither the first large-scale book digitization project (e.g., the Million Book Project has already digitized over 600,000 volumes)[3] nor the last. At the same time that Google was striking deals with libraries to digitize their collections, the Internet Archive and its partner, Yahoo! were busy recruiting members for the Open Content Alliance.[4]

The Open Content Alliance is a diverse consortium that includes cultural, nonprofit, technology, and government organizations that offer both technological expertise and resources (e.g., Adobe Systems, HP Labs, Internet Archive, MSN, Yahoo!) and rich content (e.g., Columbia University, the UK's National Archives, the National Library of Australia, Smithsonian Institution Libraries,

the University of California). It has a broad mission to "build a permanent archive of multilingual digitized text and multimedia content" and "to offer broad, public access to a rich panorama of world culture."[5]

The Open Content Alliance has launched the Open Library,[6] which, like Google Book Search, will make the full texts of large quantities of books accessible via Yahoo!'s search engine while simultaneously respecting copyright restrictions. However, unlike the Google initiative, the Open Library is committed to making the full text of every digitized book available free of charge on the Web.

The undeniably positive result of these various initiatives is that within the next decade or so the Web will be vastly enriched by the addition of a huge and freely accessible corpus of the world's literature. Unfortunately, however, unless the copyright situation improves dramatically (e.g., through the introduction of proposed new legislation for "orphan works"),[7] it seems that the corpus of literature soon to be freely available on the Web will not include any significant quantity of copyrighted material from the twentieth and twenty-first centuries.

---

1 Google Books–Library Project: http://books.google. com/googlebooks/library.html.

2 Google Books–Partner Program: http://books.google. com/googleboos/publisher.html.

3 Million Books Project Frequently Asked Questions: http://www.library.cmu.edu/Libraries/MBP_FAQ.html.

4 Open Content Alliance: http://www.opencontent alliance.org/.

5 Open Content Alliance Frequently Asked Questions: http://www.opencontentalliance.org/faq.html.

6 The Open Library: http://www.openlibrary.org/.

7 Report on Orphan Works: A Report of the Register of Copyrights, January 2006, U.S. Copyright Office. http://www.copyright.gov/orphan/. See also "Rights Metadata Made Simple," p. 63.

museum, library, and archive communities for whom metadata is really just cataloging with a different name. All the necessary standards and technology components to facilitate intracommunity knowledge sharing are now in place:

- Descriptive data structure standards for different kinds of community resource descriptions, for example, MARC,[42] Dublin Core, MODS,[43] EAD,[44] CDWA Lite,[45] and VRA Core;[46]
- Markup languages and schemas for encoding metadata in machine-readable syntaxes, for example, XML and RDF;
- Ontologies for semantic mediation between data standards, for example, CIDOC CRM and IFLA FRBRoo;[47]
- Protocols for distributed search and metadata harvesting, for example, the Z39.50 family of information retrieval protocols (Z39.50,[48] SRU/SRW[49]), SOAP,[50] and OAI-PMH.[51]

By combining these various components in imaginative ways to provide access to the rich information content found in museums, libraries, and archives, it should be possible to build a distributed global Semantic Web of digital cultural content and the appropriate vertically integrated search tools to help users find the content they are seeking therein.

---

[42] http://www.loc.gov/marc/.

[43] http://www.loc.gov/standards/mods/.

[44] http://www.loc.gov/ead/.

[45] http://www.getty.edu/research/conducting_research/standards/cdwa/cdwalite.htm.

[46] http://www.vraweb.org/projects/vracore4/index.html.

[47] http://cidoc.ics.forth.gr/frbr_inro.html.

[48] Z39.50 Maintenance Agency: http://www.loc.gov/z3950/agency/.

[49] SRU (Search/Retrieve via URL): http://www.loc.gov/standards/sru/.

[50] Simple Object Access Protocol (SOAP): http://www.w3.org/TR/2000/NOTE-SOAP-20000508/.

[51] Open Archives Initiative Protocol for Metadata Harvesting (OAH-PMH): http://www.openarchives.org/OAI/openarchivesprotocol.html.

Crosswalks, Metadata Harvesting, Federated Searching, Metasearching: Using Metadata to Connect Users and Information

Mary S. Woodley

Since the turn of the millennium, instantaneous access to a wide variety of content via the Web has ceased to be considered "bleeding-edge technology" and instead has become expected. In fact, from 2000 to the time of this writing, there has been continued exponential growth in the number of digital projects providing online access to a range of information resources: Web pages, full-text articles and books, cultural heritage resources (including images of works of art, architecture, and material culture), and other intellectual content, including born digital objects. Users increasingly expect that the Web will serve as a portal to the entire universe of knowledge. Recently, Google Scholar, Yahoo! and OCLC's WorldCat (a union catalog of the holdings of national and international libraries) have joined forces to direct users to the closest library that owns the book they are seeking, whether it is available in print or online or both.[1] Global access to the universe of traditional print materials and digital resources has become more than ever the goal of many institutions that create and/or manage digital resources.

Unfortunately, there are still no magic programming scripts that can create seamless access to the right information in the right context so that it can be efficiently retrieved and understood. At this point, most institutions (including governments, libraries, archives, museums, and commercial enterprises) have moved from in-house manual systems to automated systems in order to provide the most efficient means to control

The author would like to thank Karim Boughida of George Washington University for his invaluable input about metasearching and metadata harvesting and Diane Hillmann, of Cornell University, who graciously commented on the chapter as a whole. The author takes full responsibility for any errors or omissions.

[1] For more about the Google and WorldCat partnership, see http://scholar.google.com/scholar/libraries.html. More information about OCLC's Open WorldCat program can be found at http://www.oclc.org/worldcat/open/.

and provide access to their collections and assets.[2] Some institutions have a single information system for managing all their content; others support multiple systems that may or may not be interoperable. Individual institutions, or communities of similar institutions, have created shared metadata standards to help to organize their particular content. These standards might include elements or fields, with their definitions (also known as metadata element sets or data structure standards);[3] codified rules or best practices for recording the information with which the fields or elements are populated (data content standards); and vocabularies, thesauri, and controlled lists of terms or the actual data values that go into the data structures (data value standards).[4] The various specialized communities or knowledge domains tend to maintain their own data structure, data content, and data value standards, tailored to serve their specific types of collections and their core users. It is when communities want to share their content in a broader arena, or reuse the information for other purposes, that problems of interoperability arise. Seamless, precise retrieval of information objects formulated according to diverse sets of rules and standards is still far from a reality.

The development of sophisticated tools to enable users to discover, access, and share digital content, such as link resolvers, OAI-PMH harvesters, and the development of the Semantic Web have increased users' expectations that they will be able to search simultaneously across many different metadata structures.[5]

The goal of seamless access has motivated institutions to convert their legacy data, originally developed for in-house use, to standards more readily accessible for public display or sharing; or to provide a single interface to search many heterogeneous databases or Web resources at the same time. Metadata crosswalks are at the heart of our ability to make this possible, whether they are used to convert data to a new or different

---

[2] An excellent survey of the history and future of library automation can be found in Christine Borgman, "From Acting Locally to Thinking Globally: A Brief History of Library Automation," *Library Quarterly* 67, no. 3 (July 1997): 215–49.

[3] What determines the granularity or detail in any element will vary from standard to standard. In different systems, single instances of metadata may be referred to as fields, labels, tabs, identifiers, and so on. Margaret St. Pierre and William P. LaPlant Jr., "Issues in Crosswalking, Content Metadata Standards," in *NISO Standards*. http://www.niso.org/press/whitepapers/crsswalk.html.

[4] See the Typology of Data Standards in the first chapter of this book.

[5] The Semantic Web is a collaborative effort led by the W3C, the goal of which is to provide a common framework that will allow data to be shared and reused across various applications as well as across enterprise and community boundaries. The Semantic Web is based on common formats such as RDF (see Tony Gill's discussion in the preceding chapter), which make it possible to integrate and combine data drawn from diverse sources. http://www.w3.org/2001/sw/.

standard, to harvest and repackage data from multiple resources, to search across heterogeneous resources, or to merge diverse information resources.

Definitions and Scope

For the purposes of this chapter, "mapping" refers to the intellectual activity of comparing and analyzing two or more metadata schemas; "crosswalks" are the visual and textual product of the mapping process.
A crosswalk is a table or chart that shows the relationships and equivalencies (and highlights the inevitable gaps) between two or more metadata formats. An example of a simple crosswalk is given in table 1, where a subset of elements from four different metadata schemas are mapped to one another. Table 2 is a more detailed mapping between MARC21 and Simple Dublin Core. Note that in almost all cases there is a many-to-one relationship between the richer element set (in this example, MARC) and the simpler set (Dublin Core).

Metadata Mapping and Crosswalks

Crosswalks are used to compare metadata elements from one schema or element set to one or more other schemas. In comparing two metadata element sets or schemas, similarities and differences must be understood on multiple levels so as to evaluate the degree to which the schemas are

Table 1. **Example of a Crosswalk of a Subset of Elements from Different Metadata Schemes**

CDWA	MARC	EAD	Dublin Core
Object/Work-Type	655 Genre/form	<controlaccess><genreform>	Type
Titles or Names	24Xa Title and Title—Related Information	<unittitle>	Title
Creation–Date	260c Imprint—Date of Publication	<unitdate>	Date.Created
Creation-Creator-Identity	1XX Main Entry 7XX Added Entry	<origination><persname> <origination><corpname> <origination><famname> <controlaccess><persname> <controlaccess><corpname>	Creator
Subject Matter	520 Summary, etc. 6xx Subject Headings	 <scopecontent> <controlaccess><subject>	Subject
Current Location	852 Location	<repository><physloc>	

Table 2. **Example of a Crosswalk: MARC21 to Simple Dublin Core**

MARC Fields	Dublin Core Elements
130, 240, 245, 246	Title
100, 110, 111	Creator
100, 110, 111, 700, 710, 711*	Contributor
600, 610, 630, 650, 651, 653	Subject / Keyword
Notes 500, 505, 520, 562, 583	Description
260 $b	Publisher
581, 700 $t, 730, 787, 776	Relationship
008/ 07-10 260 $c	Date

interoperable; crosswalks are the visual representations, or "maps," that show these relationships of similarity and difference.

One definition of interoperability is "the ability of different types of computers, networks, operating systems, and applications to work together effectively, without prior communication, in order to exchange information in a useful and meaningful manner. Interoperability can be seen as having three aspects: semantic, structural and syntactic."[6] Semantic mapping is the process of analyzing the definitions of the elements or fields to determine whether they have the same or similar meanings. A crosswalk supports the ability of a search engine to query fields with the same or similar content in different databases; in other words, it supports "semantic interoperability." Crosswalks are not only important for supporting the demand for "one-stop shopping," or cross-domain searching; they are also instrumental for converting data from one format to another.[7] "Structural interoperability" refers to the presence of data models or wrappers that specify the semantic schema being used. For example, the Resource Description Framework, or RDF, is a standard that allows metadata to be defined and shared by different communities.[8] "Syntactic interoperability," also called technical interoperability, refers to the ability to communicate, transport, store, and represent metadata and other types of information between and among different systems and schemas.[9]

---

[6] DCMI Glossary. http://www.dublincore.org/documents/usageguide/glossary.shtml.

[7] Ibid. Crosswalks can be expressed or coded for machines to automate the mapping between different metadata element sets or schemas.

[8] http://www.w3.org/RDF. See also the discussion of RDF in the preceding chapter.

[9] See Paul Miller, "Interoperability Focus," http://www.ukoln.ac.uk/interop-forcus/about/.

Mapping metadata elements from different schemas is only one level of crosswalking. At another level of semantic interoperability are the *data content standards* for formulating the *data values* that populate the metadata elements, for example, rules for recording personal names or encoding standards for dates. A significant weakness of crosswalks of metadata elements alone is that results of a query will be less successful if the name or concept is expressed differently in each database. By using standardized ways to express terms and phrases for identifying people, places, corporate bodies, and concepts, it is possible to greatly improve retrieval of relevant information associated with a particular concept. Some online resources provide access to controlled terms, along with cross-references for variant forms of terms or names that point the searcher to the preferred form. This optimizes the searching and retrieval of information objects such as bibliographic records, images, and sound files. However, there is no universal authority file,[10] much less a universal set of cataloging rules that catalogers, indexers, and users consult. Each cataloging or indexing domain has developed its own cataloging rules as well as its own domain-specific thesauri or lists of terms that are designed to support the research needs of a particular community. Crosswalks have been used to migrate the *data structure* of information resources from one format to another, but only recently have there been projects to map the *data values* that populate those structures.[11] When searching many databases at once, precision and relevance become even more crucial. This is especially true if one is searching bibliographic records, records from citation databases, and full-text resources at the same time. Integrated authority control would significantly improve both retrieval and interoperability in searching disparate resources like these.

The Gale Group attempted to solve the problem of multiple subject thesauri by creating a single thesaurus and mapping the controlled vocabulary from the individual databases to their own in-house thesaurus. It is unclear to what extent the depth and coverage of the controlled terms in the individual databases are compromised by this merging.[12]

The Simple Knowledge Organization Scheme (SKOS Core) project by the W3C Semantic Web Best Practices and Deployment Working Group is a set of specifications for organizing, documenting, and publishing taxonomies, classification schemes, and controlled vocabularies,

---

[10] A virtual international authority file has been posited by Barbara Tillett, but it is far from a reality as of this writing. See B. Tillett, "A Virtual International Authority File," in *6th IFLA Council and General Conference*, August 16–25, 2001. http://www.ifla.org/IV/ifla67/papers/094-152ae.pdf.

[11] Sherry L. Vellucci, "Metadata and Authority Control," *LRTS* 44, no. 1 (January 2000): 33–43. See the Typology of Data Standards in the first chapter of this book.

[12] Jessica L. Milstead, "Cross-File Searching," *Searcher* 7, no. 1 (May 1999): 44–55.

such as thesauri, subject lists, and glossaries or terminology lists, within an RDF framework.[13] SKOS mapping is a specific application that is used to express mappings between diverse knowledge organization schemes. The National Science Digital Library's Metadata Registry is one of the first production deployments of SKOS.[14] Mapping and crosswalks of metadata elements are fairly well developed activities in the digital library world; mapping of data values is still in an early phase. But, clearly, the ability to map vocabularies (data value standards), as well as the metadata element sets (data structure standards) that are "filled" with the data values, will significantly enhance the ability of search engines to effectively conduct queries across heterogeneous databases.[15]

Syntactical interoperability is achieved by shared markup languages and data format standards that make it possible to transmit and share data between computers. For instance, in addition to being a data structure standard, MARC (Machine-Readable Cataloging Record) is the transmission format used by bibliographic utilities and libraries;[16] EAD (Encoded Archival Description) can be expressed as a DTD (document type definition) or an XML schema for archival finding aids expressed in SGML or XML; CDWA Lite is an XML schema for metadata records for works of art, architecture, and material culture; and Dublin Core metadata records can be expressed in HTML or XML.[17]

The Role of Crosswalks in Repurposing and Transforming Metadata

The process of repurposing metadata covers a broad spectrum of activities: converting or transforming records from one metadata schema to another, migrating from a legacy schema (whether standard or local) to a different schema, integrating records created according to different metadata schemas, and harvesting or aggregating metadata records that were created using a shared community standard or different metadata standards. Dushay and Hillmann note that the library community has

---

[13] See the SKOS home page at http://www.w3.org/2004/02/skos/.

[14] The NSDL metadata registry can be found at http://metadataregistry.org/.

[15] For an introduction to the SKOS Core project, see Alistar Miles, "SKOS Core: Simple Knowledge Organization for the Web," in *DC-2005 Proceedings of the International Conference on Dublin Core and Metadata Applications*. http://www.slais.ubc.ca/PEOPLE/faculty/tennis-p/dcpapers/paper01.pdf.

[16] MARC serves as a transmission standard as well as a metadata standard whose rules for content are governed by AACR. Key access points (names, subjects, titles) use values from authority files. MARC can also be expressed in XML. http://www.loc.gov/standards/marcxml///.

[17] Simple Dublin Core and Qualified Dublin Core can also be expressed in XHTML and RDF/XML. Details on encoding guidelines are available at http://dublincore.org/resources/expressions/.

an extensive and fairly successful history of aggregating metadata records (in the MARC format) created by many different libraries that share data content and data value standards (*Anglo-American Cataloguing Rules*, Library of Congress authorities) as well as a common data structure standard and transmission format (MARC). However, aggregating metadata records from different repositories may create confusing display results, especially if some of the metadata was automatically generated or created by institutions or individuals that did not follow best practices or standard thesauri and controlled vocabularies.[18]

Data conversion projects transfer the values in metadata fields or elements from one system (and often one schema) to another. Institutions convert data for a variety of reasons, for example, when upgrading to a new system, because the legacy system has become obsolete, or when the institution has decided to provide public access to some or all of its content and therefore wishes to convert from a proprietary schema to a standard schema for publishing data. Conversion is accomplished by mapping the structural elements in the older system to those in the new system. In practice, there is often not the same granularity between all the fields in the two systems, which makes the process of converting data from one system to another more complex. Data fields in the legacy database may not have been well defined, or may contain a mix of types of information. In the new database, this information may reside in separate fields. Identifying the unique information within a field to map to a separate field may not always be possible and may require manipulating the same data several times before migrating it.

Some of the common misalignments that occur when migrating data are as follows:[19]

1. There may be fuzzy matches. A metadata element in the original database does not have a perfect equivalent in the target database; for example, when mapping the CDWA element[20] "Styles/ Periods/Groups/Movements" to simple Dublin Core, we find that there is not a DC element with the exact same meaning. The Dublin Core Subject element can be used, but the semantic mapping is far from accurate, since it's the subject, not the style, that a work of art is "about."

---

[18] Naomi Dushay and Diane Hillmann, "Analyzing Metadata for Effective Use and Reuse," in *DC-2003 Proceedings of the International DCMI Metadata Conference and Workshop*. http://www.siderean.com/dc2003/501_Paper24.pdf.

[19] See the NISO white paper by Margaret St. Pierre and William P. LaPlante Jr., "Issues in Crosswalking, Content Metadata Standards" (October 1998). http://www.niso.org/press/whitepapers/crsswalk.html.

[20] CDWA stands for *Categories for the Description of Works of Art*, a standard for describing cultural objects that is maintained by the J. Paul Getty Trust. http://www.getty.edu/research/conducting_research/standards/cdwa/index.html.

2. Although some metadata standards follow the principle of a one-to-one relationship,[21] as in the case of Dublin Core, in practice many memory institutions use the same record to record information about the original object and its related image or digital surrogate, thus creating a sort of hybrid work/image or work/digital surrogate record. When migrating and harvesting data, this may pose problems if the harvester cannot distinguish between the elements that describe the original work or item and those that describe the surrogate (which is often a digital copy, full or partial, of the original item).

3. Data that exists in one metadata element in the original schema may be mapped to more than one element in the target schema. For example, data values from the CDWA Creation-Place element may be mapped to the "Subject" element and/or the "Coverage" element in Dublin Core.

4. Data in separate fields in the original schema may be in a single field in the target schema; for example, in CDWA, the birth and death dates for a "creator" are recorded in the Creator-Identity-Dates, as well as in separate fields—all apart from the creator's name. In MARC, both dates are a "subfield" in the string for the "author's" name.

5. There is no field in the target schema with an equivalent meaning, so that unrelated information may be forced into a metadata element with unrelated or only loosely related content.

6. The original "standard" is actually a mix of standards. Kurth, Ruddy, and Rupp have pointed out that even when metadata is being transformed from a single schema, it may not be possible to use the same conversion mapping for all the records that are being converted. Staff working on the Cornell University Library (CUL) projects became aware of the difficulties of "transforming" library records originally formulated in the MARC format to TEI XML headers. Not only were there subtle (and at times not so subtle) differences over time in the use of MARC, but the cataloging rules guiding how the content was entered had undergone changes from pre–*Anglo-American Cataloguing Rules* to the revised edition of AACR2.[22]

---

21 Dublin Core Abstract Model. http://dublincore.org/documents/abstract-model/#sect-3.

22 Martin Kurth, David Ruddy, and Nathan Rupp, "Repurposing MARC Metadata: Using Digital Project Experience to Develop a Metadata Management Design," *Library High Tech* 22, no. 2 (2004): 153–65. Available at lts.library.cornell.edu/lts/who/pre/upload/p153.pdf.

7. In only a few cases does the mapping work equally well in both directions, due to differences in granularity and community-specific information. (See no. 2 above.) The Getty metadata crosswalk maps in a single direction:[23] CDWA was analyzed and the other data systems were mapped to its elements. However, there are types of information that are recorded in MARC that are lost in this process; for example, the concepts of publisher and language are important in library records but are less relevant to CDWA, which focuses on one-of-a-kind cultural objects.

8. One metadata element set may have a hierarchical structure with complex relationships between elements (e.g., EAD), while the other may be a flat structure (e.g., MARC).[24]

Methods for Integrated Access/Cross-Collection Searching

Traditional Union Catalogs

The most time tested and in some ways still the most reliable way of enabling users to search across records from a variety of different institutions is the traditional union catalog. In this method, various institutions contribute records to an aggregator or service provider, preferably using a single, standard metadata schema (such as MARC for bibliographic records), a single data content standard (for libraries, AACR, to be superseded by RDA in the future), and shared controlled vocabularies (e.g., Library of Congress Subject Headings, the Library of Congress Name Authority File, *Thesaurus for Graphic Materials*, and *Art & Architecture Thesaurus*).

Within a single community, union catalogs can be created where records from different institutions can be centrally maintained and searched with a single interface, united in a single database consisting of records from different contributing institutions. This is possible because the contributing community shares the same rules for description and access and the same protocol for encoding the information. OCLC's WorldCat and RLG's RLIN[25] bibliographic file are two major union

---

[23] Metadata Standards Crosswalk: http://www.getty.edu/research/conducting_research/ standards/intrometadata/metadata_element_sets.html.

[24] See the ARTstor case study (Case Study 4) below. For other examples of crosswalk issues, see "Challenges and Issues with Metadata Crosswalks," *Online Libraries & Microcomputers*, April 2002. http://www.accessmylibrary.com/coms2/summary_0286-9128739_ITM.

[25] In spring 2006, OCLC and RLG began the process of merging their union catalogs. At the time of this writing, they had not resolved the issues involving displaying all institutional records that are clustered (RLG) or displaying the first record entered into the system with only the holdings symbols of other institutions attached (OCLC).

catalogs that make records from a wide variety of libraries available for searching from a single interface, in a single schema (MARC). There are also "local" union catalogs that aggregate records from a particular consortium or educational system; for example, the University of California and the California State Universities maintain their own union catalogs of library holdings (Melvyl and PHAROS, respectively). Interoperability is high, because of the shared schemas and rules for creating the "metadata" or cataloging records.[26]

Metadata Harvesting

A more recent model for union catalogs is to create single repositories by "harvesting" metadata records from various resources. (See Tony Gill's discussion of metadata harvesting and figure 1 in the preceding chapter.) Metadata harvesting, unlike metasearching, is not a search protocol; rather, it is a protocol that allows the gathering or collecting of metadata records from various repositories or databases; the harvested records are then "physically" aggregated in a single database, with links from individual records back to their home environments. The current standard protocol being used to harvest metadata is the OAI-PMH (Open Archives Initiative Protocol for Metadata Harvesting) Version 2.[27] The challenge has been to collect these records in such a way that they make sense to users in the union environment while maintaining their integrity and their relationship to their original context, both institutional and intellectual.

To simplify the process for implementation and to preserve interoperability, the OAI-PMH has adopted unqualified Dublin Core as its minimum metadata standard. Data providers that expose their metadata for harvesting are required to provide records in unqualified Dublin Core expressed in XML and to use UTF-8 character encoding,[28] in addition to any other metadata formats they may choose to expose. The data providers may expose all or selective metadata sets for harvesting and may also decide how rich or "lean" the individual records they make available for harvesting will be. Service providers operating downstream of the harvesting source may add value to the metadata in the form of added elements that can enhance the metadata records (such as adding audience or grade level to

---

[26] But even union catalogs consisting of records created according to a single schema (in this case, MARC) experience interoperability issues caused by changes to the standards; see no. 6 in the list of common misalignments above.

[27] The Open Archives Initiative can be found at http://www.openarchives.org/. Of particular interest is the documentation on the protocol for harvesting as well as an OAI tutorial (http://www.oaforum.org/tutorial/) and a link to the NSDL Metadata Primer (http://metamanagement.comm.nsdlib.org/outline.html).

[28] See http://unicode.org/faq/utf_bom.html#General.

educational resources). Service providers also have the potential to provide a richer contextual environment for users to find related and relevant content. Repositories using a richer, more specific metadata schema than Dublin Core (such as CDWA Lite, MARC XML, MODS, or ONIX) need to map their content to unqualified Dublin Core in order to conform to the harvesting protocol.[29] Part of the exercise of creating a crosswalk is understanding the pros and cons of mapping all the content from a particular schema or metadata element set and the institution's specific records expressed in that schema, or deciding which subset of the content should be mapped.

The pitfalls of mapping between metadata standards have been outlined above. Bruce and Hillmann established a set of criteria for measuring the quality of metadata records harvested and aggregated into a "union" collection. The criteria may be divided into two groups, one that evaluates the intellectual content of the metadata records in terms of its completeness, currency, accuracy, and provenance; and one that evaluates the metadata records from a more detailed perspective: the conformance of the metadata sets and application profiles as expected and the consistency and coherence of the data encoded in the harvested records.[30] In the context of harvesting data for reuse, Dushay and Hillmann have identified four categories of metadata problems in the second category of criteria: (1) missing data, because it was considered unnecessary by the creating institution (e.g., metadata records that do not indicate that the objects being described are maps or photographs, because they reside in a homogeneous collection where all the objects have the same format); (2) incorrect data (e.g., data that is included in the wrong metadata element or encoded improperly); (3) confusing data that uses inconsistent formatting or punctuation; and (4) insufficient data concerning the encoding schemes or vocabularies used.[31] A recent study evaluating the quality of harvested metadata found that collections from a single institution did not vary much in terms of the criteria outlined above, but the amount of "variance"

[29] See the OAI Best Practices "Multiple Metadata Formats" page, where it is stated, "Use of metadata formats in addition to Simple Dublin Core are both allowed and encouraged." http://webservices.itcs.umich.edu/mediawiki/oaibp/index.php/MultipleMetadataFormats. A recent experiment in harvesting a richer metadata set (CDWA Lite) within a Dublin Core "wrapper," along with a related OAI "resource" (in this case, a digital image) is discussed below in Case Study 4.

[30] Thomas R. Bruce and Diane I. Hillmann, "The Continuum of Metadata Quality: Defining, Expressing, Exploiting," in *Metadata in Practice*, ed. Diane Hillmann and Elaine L. Westbrooks (Chicago: American Library Association, 2004), pp. 238–56.

[31] Naomi Dushay and Diane Hillmann, "Analyzing Metadata for Effective Use and Reuse," in *DC-2003 Proceedings of the International DCMI Metadata Conference and Workshop.* http://www.siderean.com/dc2003/501_Paper24.pdf.

increased dramatically when the aggregations of harvested metadata came from many different institutions.[32]

Tennant echoes the argument that the problem may be mapping to simple Dublin Core. He suggests that both data providers and service providers consider exposing and harvesting records encoded in metadata schemas that are richer and more appropriate to the collections at hand than unqualified Dublin Core. Tennant argues that the metadata harvested should be as granular as possible and that the service provider should transform and normalize data such as dates, which are expressed in a variety of encoding schemes by the various data providers.[33]

Like the traditional union catalog model, the metadata harvesting model creates a single "place" for searching instead of providing real-time decentralized or distributed searching of diverse resources, as in the metasearching model. In the harvesting model, to facilitate searching, an extra "layer" is added to the aggregation of harvested records; this layer manages the mapping and searching of heterogeneous metadata records within a single aggregated resource. Godby, Young, and Childress have suggested a model for creating a repository of metadata crosswalks that could be exploited by OAI harvesters. Documentation about the mapping would be associated with the standard used by the data providers, and the metadata presented by the service providers would be encoded in METS.[34] This would provide a mechanism for facilitating the transformation of OAI-harvested metadata records by service providers.

Metasearching

The number of metadata standards continues to grow, and it is unrealistic to think that records from every system can be converted to a common standard that will satisfy both general and domain-specific user needs. An alternative is to maintain the separate metadata element sets and schemas that have been developed to support the needs of specific communities and offer a search interface that allows users to search simultaneously across a range of heterogeneous databases. This can be achieved through a variety of methods and protocols that are generally grouped under the rubric *metasearch*.

---

[32] Sarah L. Shreeves et al., "Is 'Quality' Metadata 'Shareable' Metadata? The Implications of Local Metadata Practices for Federated Collections," in *ACRL Twelfth National Conference, Minneapolis, MN, 2005 April 9*, pp. 223–37. http://www.ala.org/ala/acrl/acrlevents/shreeves05.pdf.

[33] Roy Tennant, "Bitter Harvest: Problems & Suggested Solutions for OAI-PMH Data & Service Providers." http://www.cdlib.org/inside/projects/harvesting/bitter_harvest.html.

[34] Carol Jean Godby, Jeffrey A. Young, and Eric Childress, "A Repository of Metadata Crosswalks," *D-Lib Magazine* 10, no. 12 (December 2004). http://www.dlib.org/dlib/december04/godby/12godby.html.

Many different terms and definitions have been used for meta-searching, including broadcast searching, parallel searching, and search portal. I follow the definition given by the NISO MetaSearch Initiative: "search and retrieval to span multiple databases, sources, platforms, protocols, and vendors at one time."[35]

The best-known and most widely used metasearch engines in the library world are based on the Z39.50 protocol.[36] The development of this protocol was initiated to allow simultaneous searching of the Library of Congress, OCLC's WorldCat, and the RLIN bibliographic file to create a virtual union catalog and to allow libraries to share their cataloging records. With the advent of the Internet, the protocol was extended to enable searching of abstracting and indexing services and full-text resources when they were Z39.50 compliant. Some people touted Z39.50 as the holy grail of search: one-stop shopping with seamless access to all authoritative information. At the time of its implementation, Z39.50 had no competitors, but it was not without its detractors.[37]

The library community is split over the efficacy of meta-searching. When is "good enough" really acceptable? Often, the results created through a keyword query of multiple heterogeneous resources have high recall and little precision, leaving the patron at a loss as to how to proceed. Users who are used to Web search engines will often settle for the first hits generated from a metasearch, regardless of their suitability for their information needs. Authors have pointed to Google's "success" to reaffirm the need for federated searching without referring to any studies that evaluate the satisfaction of researchers.[38] A recent preliminary study conducted by Lampert and Dabbour on the efficacy of federated searching laments that until recently studies have focused on the technical aspects of metasearch, without considering student search and selection habits or the impact of federated searching on information literacy.[39]

What are some of the issues related to metasearch? In some interfaces, search results may be displayed in the order retrieved, or by relevance, either sorted by categories or integrated. As we know, relevance

---

[35] NISO MetaSearch Initiative; http://www.niso.org/committees/MS_initiative.html.

[36] For a history of the development of the standard, see Clifford A. Lynch, "The Z39.50 Retrieval Standard. Part 1: A Strategic View of Its Past, Present and Future," *D-Lib Magazine* (April 1997). http://www.dlib.org/dlib/april97/04lynch.html.

[37] Roy Tennant, "Interoperability: The Holy Grail," *Library Journal*, July 1, 1998. http://www.libraryjournal.com/article/CA156495. For Tennant, interoperability was the holy grail; for others, it is Z39.50 and its successor, ZING.

[38] Judy Luther, "Trumping Google? Metasearching's Promise," *Library Journal*, October 1, 2003. Available at http://www.libraryjournal.com/article/CA322627.html.

[39] Lynn D. Lampert and Katherine S. Dabbour, "Librarian Perspectives on Teaching Metasearch and Federated Search Technologies," *Internet Reference Services Quarterly* 12, nos. 3–4 (2007): 253–78.

ranking often has little or nothing to do with what the searcher is really seeking. Having the choice of searching a single database or multiple databases allows users to take advantage of the specialized indexing and controlled vocabulary of a single database or to cast a broader net, with less vocabulary control.

There are several advantages of a single gateway, or portal, to information. Users do not always know which of the many databases they have access to will provide them with the best information. Libraries have attempted to list databases by categories and provide brief descriptions; but users tend not to read lists, and this type of "segregation" of resources neglects the interdisciplinary nature of research. Few users have the tenacity to read lengthy alphabetic lists of databases or to ferret out databases relevant to their queries when they are buried in lengthy menus. On the other hand, users can be overwhelmed by large result sets from federated searches and may have difficulty finding what they need, even if the results are sorted by relevance.[40]

As of this writing, the commercial metasearch engines for libraries are still using the Z39.50 protocol to search across multiple repositories simultaneously.[41] In simple terms, this protocol allows two computers to communicate in order to retrieve information; a client computer will query another computer, a server, which provides a result. Libraries employ this protocol to support searching of other library catalogs as well as abstracting and indexing services and full-text repositories. Searches and results are restricted to databases that are Z39.50 compatible. The results that users see from searching multiple repositories through a single interface and those achieved when searching their native interfaces individually may differ significantly, for the following reasons:

- The way the server interprets the query from the client. This is especially the case when the query uses multiple keywords. Some databases will search a keyword string as a phrase; others automatically add the Boolean operator "and" between keywords; yet others automatically add the Boolean operator "or."
- How a specific person, place, event, object, idea, or concept is expressed in one database may not be how it is expressed in

---

[40] Terence K. Huwe, "New Search Tools for Multidisciplinary Digital Libraries," *Online* 23, no. 2 (March 1999): 67–70.

[41] The protocol is a NISO standard, http://www.niso.org/z39.50/z3950.html, which is maintained by the Library of Congress, http://www.loc.gov/z3950/agency, and ISO standard http://www.iso.org/iso/en/CatalogueDetailPage.CatalogueDetail?CSNUMBER=27446. A good history of Z39.50 was published in the ALCTS series, From Catalog to Gateway: William E. Moen, *Interoperability and Z39.50 Profiles: The Bath and U.S. Profiles for Library Applications.*

another. This is the vocabulary issue, which has a significant impact on search results when querying single resources (e.g., the name or term that the user employs may or may not match the name or term employed in the database to express the same concept). This is exacerbated when querying multiple resources, where different name forms and terms proliferate.

- Metasearch engines vary in how results are displayed. Some display results in the order in which they were retrieved; others, by the database in which they were found; still others, sorted by date or integrated and ranked by relevance. The greater the number of results, the more advantages may be derived from sorting by relevance and/or date.[42]

ZING (Z39.50 International: Next Generation)[43] strives to improve the functionality and flexibility of the Z39.50 protocol while making the implementation of Z39.50 easier for vendors and data publishers in the hope of encouraging its adoption. ZING incorporates a series of services. One is a Web service for searching and retrieving (SRW) from a client to a server using SOAP (Simple Object Access Protocol), which uses XML for the exchange of structured information in a distributed environment.[44] Another is SRU, a standard search protocol for the Web that searches and retrieves through a URI.[45] Although the development of ZING holds the promise of better performance and interoperability, as of this writing it has not been widely adopted.

The limitations of Z39.50 have encouraged the development of alternative solutions to federated searching to improve the way results are presented to users. One approach is the XML Gateway (MXG), which allows queries in an XML format from a client to generate result sets from a server in an XML format.[46] Another approach used by metasearch engines when the database does not support Z39.50 relies on HTTP parsing, or "screen scraping." In this approach, the search retrieves an HTML page that is parsed and submitted to the user in the retrieved set. Unfortunately, this approach requires a high level of maintenance, as the target databases are continually changing and the level of accuracy in retrieving content varies among the databases.

[42] Tamar Sadeh, "The Challenge of Metasearching," *New World Library* 105, nos. 1198–99 (2004): 104–12.

[43] http://www.loc.gov/z3950/agency/zing/.

[44] SOAP is a protocol using XML that is used for exchanging structured data in a distributed environment. http://www.w3.org/TR/soap12-part1/.

[45] http://www.loc.gov/standards/sru/.

[46] NISO Metasearch Initiative, Standards Committee BC, Task Group 3, *Metasearch XML Gateway Implementors Guide*, July 12, 2005. http://www.niso.org/standards/resources/MI-MXG_v0_3.pdf.

Table 3. **Methods for Enabling Integrated Access/Cross-Collection Searching**

Method	Description	Examples
Federated searching of physically aggregated contributed metadata records	Records from various data providers are aggregated in a single database, in a single metadata schema (either in the form contributed, e.g., in the MARC format, or "massaged" by the aggregator into a common schema), and searched in a single database with a single protocol. The service provider preprocesses the contributed data prior to it being searched by users and stores it locally. For records to be added or updated, data providers must contribute fresh records, and aggregators must batch process and incorporate the new and updated records into the union catalog.	Traditional union catalogs such as OCLC's WorldCat and the Online Archive of California (OAC); "local" or consortial union catalogs such as Ohio-Link (a consortium of Ohio's college and university libraries and the State Library of Ohio) and Melvyl (the catalog of the University of California libraries)
Federated searching of physically aggregated harvested metadata records	Records expressed in a standard metadata schema (e.g., Dublin Core) are made available by data providers on specially configured servers. Metadata records are harvested, batch processed, and made available by service providers from a single database. Metadata records usually contain a link back to the original records in their home environment, which may be in a different schema than the one used for the harvested records. The service provider preprocesses the contributed data prior to it being searched by users and stores it locally. In order for records to be added or updated, data providers must post fresh metadata records, and service providers must reharvest, batch process, and integrate the new and updated records into the union database.	OAI-harvested union catalogs such as the National Science Digital Library (NSDL), OAIster, the Sheet Music Consortium, and the UIUC Digital Gateway to Cultural Heritage Materials
Metasearch of distributed meta-data records	Diverse databases on diverse platforms with diverse metadata schemas are searched in real time via one or more protocols. The service provider does not preprocess or store data but rather processes data only when a user launches a query. Fresh records are always available because searching is in real time, in a distributed environment.	Arts and Humanities Data Service, Boston College CrossSearch, Cornell University Find Articles search service, University of Notre Dame Article Quick-Search, University of Michigan Library Quick Search, University of Minnesota Libraries MNCAT

The key to improvement may lie in the implementation of multiple protocols rather than a single protocol. As of this writing, some vendors are combining Z39.50 and XML Gateway techniques to increase the number of "targets," or servers, that can be queried in a single search.[47]

Case Studies

Each instance of data conversion, transformation, metasearching, or metadata harvesting will bring its own unique set of issues. Below are examples of projects that illustrate the complexities and pitfalls of using crosswalks and metadata mapping to convert existing metadata records from one schema to another, to enhance existing records, or to support cross-collection searching.

---

[47] Ex Libris's MetaLib is one of the products that uses this combined techniques approach.

Case Study 1: Repurposing Metadata. Links to ONIX metadata added to MARC records.

In 2001 a task force was created by the Cataloging and Classification: Access and Description Committee, an Association for Library Collections & Technical Services (ALCTS) committee under the aegis of the American Library Association (ALA), to review a standard developed by the publishing industry and to evaluate the usefulness of data in records produced by publishers to enhance the bibliographic records used by libraries. The task force reviewed and analyzed the ONIX (Online Information Exchange) element set[48] and found that some of the metadata elements developed to help bookstores increase sales could have value for the library user as well.[49] In response, the Library of Congress directed the Bibliographic Enrichment Advisory Team (BEAT) to repurpose data values from three metadata elements supplied by publishers in the ONIX format—tables of contents, descriptions, and sample texts from published books—to enhance the metadata in MARC records for the same works. The ONIX metadata is stored on servers at the Library of Congress and is accessed via hyperlinks in the corresponding MARC records,[50] as shown in figure 1. In this way, ONIX metadata originally created to manage business assets and to provide information to bookstores that would help increase book sales has been used to enhance the bibliographic records used by libraries to provide information for users so that they can more easily evaluate the particular publication.

Lessons Learned

Consistently recorded, reliable metadata can be reused and combined with metadata records that have been created according to different standards to create richer, more informative information objects. The ONIX and MARC standards are created by and serve two different communities that manage the same resources for different purposes. Librarians are becoming aware of the value of information beyond traditional bibliographic description as exemplified by MARC records created according to AACR. Individuals seeking information may find it valuable to see detailed publisher descriptions that often parallel dust jacket summaries, information about an author, and awards given to an author or publica-

---

[48] See http://www.editeur.org/onix.html.

[49] The full report can be found at http://www.libraries.psu.edu/tas/jca/ccda/tf-onix1.html. The crosswalk between ONIX and MARC21 is at http://www.loc.gov/marc/onix2marc.html.

[50] Information and documentation can be found at http://www.loc.gov/catdir/beat/. The announcement of the ONIX project is available at http://www.loc.gov/catdir/beat/beat_report.1.2001.html.

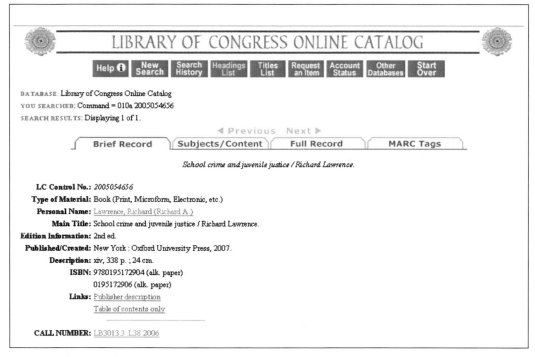

Figure 1. **MARC Record (Brief Display) with Embedded Links to ONIX Metadata (Publisher Description and Table of Contents)**

tion. With the development of Web 2.0 tools,[51] library catalogs will be able to better exploit more recent forms of metadata such as social tagging, folksonomies, and user reviews, in addition to the information provided by publishers in the ONIX format.

Case Study 2: Conversion and Migration from a Proprietary Schema to a Standard Schema. Records for auction catalogs created in SCIPIO converted into MARC records.

A special database of auction catalogs for art and rare book sales was created in 1980 by the Research Libraries Group (RLG). For this database, called SCIPIO (Sales Catalog Index Project Input Online), the museums and libraries that were members of the RLG consortium provided records for auction catalogs that followed practices that differed significantly from the rules used by libraries (AACR); the records were not encoded in the MARC format but in a proprietary format optimized specifically for

---

[51] See Tim O'Reilly, "What Is Web 2.0: Design Patterns and Business Models for the Next Generation of Software." http://www.oreillynet.com/pub/a/oreilly/tim/news/2005/09/30/what-is-web-20.html.

describing auction catalogs. The SCIPIO Advisory Group met in 1997 to form a task force to review RLG's plan to convert the SCIPIO records for auction catalogs to the MARC format.[52] Converting the SCIPIO records to the MARC format would mean that library systems could integrate them into their OPACs, making it easier for users to find the auction catalogs; many users of the OPACs might not be aware of the separate SCIPIO database. The charge of the task force was to review the proposed mapping of the metadata elements of the existing auction catalog records to the fields (i.e., metadata elements) in the MARC format. Although the metadata elements migrated in 1998, SCIPIO's rules for authority control remained unchanged until 2002.[53]

One of the main obstacles to full integration of the auction catalogs in the RLIN bibliographic file was the way in which the names of the auction houses and the names of sellers had been recorded in the SCIPIO records. In the auction catalog database, there was no authority control for the names of the individuals, families, or corporate bodies that were selling objects through the auction houses. Authority control did exist for the names of the auction houses themselves, but these were at a level of specificity that did not correspond to the Library of Congress Subject Headings (LCSH). Because the titles of auction catalogs tend to be very generic (e.g., *18th & 19th Century Furniture, Decorations, Tapestries and Carpets*), it is necessary to include the most specific name for each auction house in order to unambiguously identify a particular auction catalog. The practice of the library community, on the other hand, had been to conflate the names of the individual auction houses; for example, *Sotheby's New York* and *Sotheby's Los Angeles* had been subsumed as cross-references under *Sotheby's* in LCSH. This created a problem when the auction catalog records were integrated into library catalogs: the headings for auction houses found in the auction catalog records that had been migrated from SCIPIO did not match the headings in the Library of Congress authority records; instead, they corresponded to cross-references. The conflict was eventually resolved by updating the equivalent Library of Congress authority form to match the SCIPIO headings.[54]

Lessons Learned

This case illustrates the problems faced when the level of granularity of records created according to different schemas is significantly different.

---

[52] Deborah Kempe, "SCIPIO Art and Rare Books Catalog File: Perspective from a Valued User and Contributor," *RLIN Focus* 40 (October 1999). http://www.rlg.org/legacy/r-focus/i40.scipio.html/.

[53] Kay Downey, "SCIPIO Flips to the Library of Congress Name Authority File," *RLIN Focus* 56 (June 21, 2002). http://www.rlg.org/r-focus/i56.html#scipio/.

[54] Ibid.

Even more important, it illustrates the problems that result in mapping metadata records that have been created according to different data content standards (in this case, "local" rules for SCIPIO, and AACR for MARC) and using names and terms taken from different data value standards (the SCIPIO authority for names of auction houses vs. LCSH; in the case of the seller names in the SCIPIO records, no data value standard vs. LCSH). In short, metadata elements as well as the values with which they are populated present a range of issues related to mapping.

Case Study 3: Transformation of Museum Metadata Records to Dublin Core

A pioneering project in metadata for museums, the Consortium for the Computer Interchange of Museum Information (CIMI), was founded in 1990 to promote the creation of standards for sharing cultural information electronically.[55] In 1998 CIMI designed a project to map museum data to unqualified Dublin Core.[56] The main goal of this project was to test the efficacy of automating conversion of existing data from museums to a more Web-friendly metadata standard, that is, to Dublin Core, with as little human intervention as possible.

The test bed demonstrated the pitfalls of migrating between two different metadata standards whose granularity and purposes differ significantly. It provided an excellent example of how difficult it is to map data that resides in very specific, narrowly defined fields to a schema that lacks the same depth and specificity. In some cases, during the mapping process, data was mapped to inappropriate elements or duplicated in two different elements. For example, since museums record subject information in a single field without subfield coding, a string like "baroque dance" was mapped to both the Dublin Core *coverage.temporal* metadata element and the Dublin Core *coverage.topical* element. There are two ways to look at this dilemma. The first is that there is not a computer program sophisticated enough to be able to deconstruct textual strings into their component parts (temporal, topical, and geographic) for migrating to the appropriate separate metadata elements in the target schema. The second is that migrating the same complex subject strings into separate fields, resulting in a duplication of the same data values in more than one meta-

---

55 The CIMI project ceased as of December 15, 2003. The original CIMI Web site and documentation are no longer available, but some of the original documentation can still be found at http://www.cni.org/pub/CIMI/framework.html; and older documents are archived through the WayBackMachine at http://web.archive.org/web/*/http://www .cimi.org.

56 The Dublin Core element set is NISO standard Z39.85: http://www.niso .org/standards/resources/Z39-85.pdf.

data element, does not necessarily aid the user in finding and retrieving content; it does result in what appears to be a "cluttered" record, with redundant data values.

Lessons Learned

When moving from a complex, rich metadata scheme to a simple scheme that lacks the same degree of granularity, information will inevitably be lost. One cannot expect that indexing and retrieval using the simpler metadata scheme will be able to reproduce the power and precision of the original. The purpose of the metadata scheme to which the data is mapped must be judged in its own context: does it serve the new purpose (e.g., federation with other resources, harvestability) well, or at least well enough?

Case Study 4: Getty Museum, Getty Research Institute, and ARTstor. OAI harvesting of cultural heritage metadata and images.

Cataloging Cultural Objects (CCO)[57] is a data content standard designed to provide rules and guidelines for describing cultural materials (including art, architecture, and material culture) and their visual (including digital) surrogates. CCO was conceived in 1999 and was published as a detailed manual, with cataloging examples, in summer 2006 by the American Library Association. The need for a transmission standard to express and disseminate metadata records informed by the rules in CCO led to the creation of the CDWA Lite XML schema, which in turn is based on *Categories for the Description of Works of Art.*[58]

Lessons learned from the experience of the CIMI testbed and a careful analysis carried out by the Getty Research Institute and the J. Paul Getty Museum when they were asked to contribute records and images to ARTstor[59] showed that Dublin Core and MODS were not sufficient or appropriate schemas for expressing the kind of information that is typically recorded by museums and image archives. The Getty proposed another approach—development of a community-specific schema based on existing best practices and the real-life data that is needed by museums and other repositories—that would enhance the process of making the existing records from image archive databases and museum collection

---

[57] Documentation is available on the Web on the home page of the project: http://www.vraweb.org/ccoweb/.

[58] The schema and data dictionary are available at http://www.getty.edu/research/ conducting_research/standards/cdwa/cdwalite.html.

[59] See http://www.artstor.org.

management systems available to a broad audience.[60] In addition, rather than copy image files (in OAI parlance, "resources") to hard drives or some other cumbersome form of delivery, in this project the images related to the metadata records were also harvested.[61]

In 2005–6 the Getty Trust partnered with ARTstor to test the efficacy of converting and harvesting metadata records generated from existing databases for inclusion in ARTstor's Image Gallery, using a community-specific metadata schema. The Getty Museum and the Getty Research Institute, the data providers, worked with ARTstor, the service provider, to develop an XML schema that could be used with OAI-PMH to provide harvestable versions of both metadata records and their corresponding images ("resources," in OAI parlance). The schema that was developed, CDWA Lite, is a subset of the full CDWA element set, expressed in XML. This "light" version comprises 22 of the more than 300 elements and subelements that make up *Categories for the Description of Works of Art* (CDWA);[62] only 9 of the 22 high-level elements are required. The objective of the project was to develop a replicable way for museums and other holders of visual materials to share the most up-to-date, authoritative versions of the descriptive metadata and digital surrogates relating to their collections that would be less labor-intensive and repetitive than previous consortial methodologies such as the one that had been used by AMICO.[63] To expedite the process, the schema was optimized to work with OAI-PMH, which at the time (and at the time of this writing) was the most well tested, reliable protocol for metadata harvesting.[64]

---

[60] See Murtha Baca, "CCO and CDWA Lite: Complementary Data Content and Data Format Standards for Art and Material Culture Information," in a special issue of the *VRA Bulletin* titled *Creating Shareable Metadata:CCO and the Standards Landscape* 34, no. 1 (Spring 2007).

[61] The Open Archives Initiative Object Reuse and Exchange (OAI-ORE) project seeks to develop standards and mechanisms for "compound information objects" (e.g., metadata records and related "resources" such as digital images) to be expressed, shared, and harvested. See http://www.openarchives.org/ore/.

[62] CDWA articulates a conceptual framework, gives a comprehensive list of metadata elements, and provides detailed guidelines for describing and accessing information about works of art, architecture, other material culture, groups and collections of works, and related images. See http://www.getty.edu/research/conducting_research/standards/cdwa/index.html.

[63] The Art Museum Image Consortium, which ceased operation in June 2005. See http://www.amico.org/.

[64] See Karim B. Boughida, "CDWA Lite for Cataloging Cultural Objects (CCO): A New XML Schema for the Cultural Heritage Community," in *Humanities, Computers and Cultural Heritage: Proceedings of the XVI International Conference of the Association for History and Computing (September 2005)* (Amsterdam: Royal Netherlands Academy of Arts and Sciences, 2005), pp. 14–17. http://www.knaw.nl/publicaties/pdf/20051064.pdf.

Two collections were chosen for the project with ARTstor: records of the Getty Museum paintings that are on public display in the galleries and records of images of European tapestries in the Photo Study Collection of the Getty Research Institute. In reviewing their paintings records, the Getty Museum made the decision to provide "core" records—that is, the minimal amount of data necessary to unambiguously identify those works. This decision was informed by the assumption that the inclusion of the URL (encoded in the "linkResource" element in the CDWA Lite XML schema) to the Getty site in the ARTstor record would link the user back to a fuller description of the object, as well as additional historical and contextual information and images that had been developed to enhance the experience of nonexperts viewing collections objects on the Getty Web site. Metadata elements that are typically included in museum collection management systems but are not considered "core" and/or are not deemed appropriate for display to the public are not part of the XML schema; these elements include the exhibition history of the object, the physical location of the object in the museum's galleries, and other administrative or confidential information such as the amount that was paid for the object. Fortunately, the Getty Museum uses CDWA as the basis of the data dictionary for its collection management system, a relational database system with a built-in thesaurus module. The museum's in-house cataloging guidelines are close to the CCO guidelines, but some of the data needed to be massaged during the export process, because most of it had been recorded before the publication of CCO. For instance, the object type in the Getty Museum system uses the plural form (*paintings*, not *painting*) and therefore is noncompliant with the CCO standard. A careful analysis of the existing data and a good understanding of both the rules for the schema and the CCO rules for recording data made it possible in most cases for scripts to be written that would make the necessary changes to the data as entered during the process of converting the data from its native form in the collection management system into OAI-harvestable XML records.

Migrating the tapestry records from the Getty Research Institute's Photo Study Collection was a more complex process, since the records had been created according to a nonstandard, locally developed schema that did not conform to CDWA or any other published standard; however, many of the elements in the local schema were easily mappable to CDWA. The records for the tapestries reside in a flat-file database system that offers standard export capabilities and authority control.[65] The working group in this case approached the mapping differently. They chose to map as much as possible from the Getty Research Institute's tapestries records into the CDWA Lite schema, whereas the museum team chose to map only the core elements. The reason for this is that the museum offers very rich information, and often multiple images, on

Web pages that are publicly accessible (via the Visible Web), whereas the tapestry records and images are only accessible as part of a proprietary database that is not indexable by commercial search engines (they are hidden in the Deep Web). Thus the staff of the Getty Research Institute wanted to make available as much information as possible through ARTstor (and eventually other service providers), since they realized that because their database could not be searched from Google or other search engines, many users would not be aware of its existence. Although most of the information in the very rich Photo Study Collection records was successfully migrated to the CDWA Lite schema, the fact that the more than 55 fields in a tapestry record had to be shoehorned into the 22 CDWA Lite metadata elements necessarily resulted in some of the issues described in the preceding case study, and in the list on pages 44–46. Values from some fields from the local database (e.g., "Weaving Center") were easily mappable to the appropriate CDWA Lite element (in this case, the "creationLocation" attribute of the "Location" element), while other local fields (e.g., "Shelf Location") did not map to any element in the schema. It was not deemed necessary to publish this type of detailed information in the union catalog environment; part of the thought process when mapping metadata for conversion to a standard schema and contribution to a federated resource is determining what elements should be mapped to the published schema.

Another task that arose in the process of mapping and converting both the Getty Museum and the Getty Research Institute Photo Study Collection data was the mapping and conversion of diacritics to Unicode UTF-8,[66] which is required by the OAI protocol.

Lessons Learned

Consistently recorded, standards-based metadata is much easier to map, convert, and disseminate than "proprietary" metadata that does not comply with published standards. Loss of some metadata elements in the mapping process is not a problem, especially if the user has the ability to link back to the fuller original metadata record in its "home" environment. Metadata mapping and harvesting gives data providers the option to provide leaner or fuller versions of their records to service providers,

---

[65] An unfortunate side effect of publishing metadata records from a database system with authority control is that in the process of "flattening out" the interrelated data from the original information system to create what is essentially an XML document, the power of the authority file is destroyed. In general, only one data value/access point, the preferred or display name or term, is encoded in the harvestable metadata record; the additional access points provided by variant names or terms, more generic or more specific names or terms, etc., are lost.

[66] See http://www.unicode.org/versions/Unicode4.0.0/.

depending on the nature of their records, how they are made available on the data providers' home sites, and how much or how little data (and related resources) the data providers choose to contribute to the union environment.

Conclusion

The technological universe of crosswalks, mapping, federated searching of heterogeneous databases, and aggregating metadata sets into single repositories is rapidly changing. Crosswalks and metadata mapping are still at the heart of data conversion projects and semantic interoperability, which enable searching across heterogeneous resources. Inherently, there will always be limitations to crosswalks; there is rarely a one-to-one correspondence between metadata standards, even when one standard is a subset of another. Mapping the elements or fields of metadata systems is only one piece of the picture. Crosswalks such as SKOS, providing maps of data values from various thesauri, taxonomies, and classification schemes will further enhance searchers' ability to retrieve the most precise, relevant search results. As the number and size of online resources increase, the ability to refine searches and to use controlled vocabularies and thesauri as "searching assistants" will become increasingly important.

Rights Metadata Made Simple

Maureen Whalen

There are three common reactions when the issue of rights metadata arises:

1. "It's too complicated and overwhelming."

2. "We don't have the staff or the money."

3. "It's not the library's [or archive's, or museum's] job; it's up to users to figure out rights information if they want to publish something from our collections."

Here are some reasoned responses:

1. Yes, rights metadata can be complicated and overwhelming, but so is knitting a cardigan sweater until one simplifies the project by mastering a few basic techniques and following the instructions step-by-step.

2. Your institution is probably already spending staff time and money on rights research. Capturing rights metadata in a shared information system as a routine, programmatic activity with structured data rules and values and an established work flow should not cost any more than ad hoc rights research, and it will provide longer-lasting benefits.

3. In a world where "if it's not digital, it doesn't exist," libraries, archives, and museums have new roles with respect to their users, as well as the creators and authors of the works in their collections. Moreover, cultural heritage institutions need rights information for their own uses of the works in their collections. Rights metadata is not just about compliance with intellectual property laws; it is also about being responsible stewards of the works in our collections and the digital surrogates of those works that we create—and in a digital world, it is crucial to a memory institution's broader mission of collection, preservation, and access.

Usable, shareable, repurposable rights metadata can be obtained by capturing the following core information:[1]

1. **The name of the creator** of the work or image, including the **nationality** and **date of birth**, and the **date of death**, if applicable. Ideally, this information should be copied automatically from an authority file. (*Generally, the "work" is the original work in the institution's collection and not a digital surrogate. If the institution wants to create a rights metadata record for the digital surrogate, the approach described here would be valid, provided that the digital surrogate is described and differentiated from the original work.*)

2. **The year the work was created.** The year of creation may not be the year of publication. When two different dates exist, they should be identified separately. If the publication date is known, it should be recorded in the "publication status" field.

3. **Copyright status** (*one of the following five options can be selected from a controlled picklist by staff tasked with recording rights metadata*):
   - **Copyright owned by the institution.** The copyright is assumed valid and is owned by the institution that holds the work.
   - **Copyright owned by a third party**. The copyright is valid and is owned by someone or some entity other than the holding institution. If known, capture the name of the third party in a database field/metadata element designated for that purpose.[2]

---

[1] These suggestions for a simplified rights metadata approach are based on required rights metadata recommendations for copyrightMD, an XML schema for rights metadata developed by the California Digital Library (CDL). The copyrightMD schema is designed for incorporation with other XML schemas for descriptive and structural metadata (e.g., CDWA Lite, MARC XML, METS, MODS). See http://www.cdlib.org/inside/projects/rights/schema/. See also Karen Coyle, "Descriptive Metadata for Copyright Status," *First Monday* 10, no. 10 (October 2005). http://www.firstmonday.org/issues/issue10_10/coyle/index.html.

   N.B. The title of the work is not identified here as a rights metadata element per se; it is assumed that the title would be included in any metadata schema used to describe the work, and thus that element could be copied from the descriptive metadata record into the rights metadata schema in an automated manner.

[2] There may be certain conditions under which a license for certain specified uses of the work may have been granted to the institution. A license is not the same as ownership. If desired, when the copyright is known to be owned by a third party, the picklist could include an option for "license granted to the institution"; such a notation by itself, however, would not

- **Public domain.** If the work is determined to be in the public domain, it is helpful to identify the year in which the work entered (or will enter) the public domain, if known.
- **Orphan work.** This is a work that may be protected by copyright law but for which the copyright owner or claimant cannot be identified or located.
- **Not researched.**

4. **Publication status** (*one of the following four options can be selected from a controlled picklist by staff tasked with recording rights metadata*):
   - **Published.** Include date, if known. Publication is defined in the Copyright Act as "the distribution of copies . . . of a work to the public by sale or other transfer of ownership, or by rental, lease, or lending." Note that the offer to distribute copies, including the original work even if there is only one copy of it, constitutes publication.[3]
   - **Unpublished.** Some materials such as manuscripts and correspondence may be easily determined to be unpublished. Other works, however, such as speeches or paintings that are known to the public can still be considered "unpublished" under the Copyright Act definition.
   - **Unknown.** It is sometimes difficult to determine whether or not a work has been published, particularly for photographs of which there may be multiple prints or for manuscripts from which a work was later published.
   - **Not researched.**

5. **Date that rights research was conducted** (*if there are multiple dates on which rights research was conducted, best practice would be to include all of those dates, along with the initials of the researcher(s)*).

Gathering rights metadata and including it in an institutional information system or database[4] will allow users with some basic copyright understanding to make thoughtful judgments about how the law may affect

---

be adequate to describe the various rights granted, or denied, or the specific term during which the license is valid, so a review of the specific licensed rights would be necessary.

[3] 17 USC § 101.

[4] There is increasing discussion about embedding rights metadata in the same file as the digital surrogate, thus avoiding the problem of two digital files that can and often do get separated during transmission. As of this writing, embedding rights metadata has been done only under limited circumstances and the software necessary to embed the data and provide users with access to it using a free, downloadable reader is not yet widely available.

use of the work in accordance with a legal exception.[5] It may also help to guide determinations about how easy or how difficult it might be to obtain permission, if needed.

Table 1 gives specific examples of rights metadata for works in the public domain and works that are under copyright. Here are some examples of how the rights metadata elements articulated here can be applied in day-to-day decision making:[6]

- Knowing the birth and death dates of the creator, or the year(s) in which the work was created and published, will allow for quick calculations about the copyright term for the work. To do the analysis and arithmetic, follow Peter Hirtle's excellent chart, *Copyright Term and the Public Domain in the United States.*[7] Note: There are slightly different rules for works of foreign (non-U.S.) origin, including restoration of copyrights in works of foreign origin that may have been in the public domain for a period of time before restoration; that is why it is good practice to identify the nationality of the creator, if known.
- Unpublished works tend to have longer copyright terms than published works; therefore, if the work is assumed to be unpublished, the term of copyright protection should be calculated in accordance with the formula for unpublished works.
- While the Copyright Act specifically states that unpublished works qualify for fair use, courts tend to protect the creator's right to decide about first publication, so the standard for fair use of unpublished works is usually higher than for published materials.[8]

---

[5] The U.S. Copyright Act includes a number of limitations on (rights holders') exclusive rights. The most well known of these limitations is fair use (Section 107 of the Act), whereby use of copyrighted works without permission of the rights holder is permitted if the use meets the statutory four-factor test. Another important exception applies to libraries and archives (Section 108 of the Act). Under this exception, libraries and archives are permitted to make copies of works in their collections under certain circumstances without permission of the rights holder, including replacement copies of published works, preservation and security copies for unpublished works, and copies for users provided that the copy becomes the property of the user and is for private study, scholarship, or research.

[6] Examples include assumptions based on U.S. copyright law; examples and assumptions for non-U.S. jurisdictions are not provided here.

[7] Available at http://www.copyright.cornell.edu/training/Hirtle_Public_Domain.htm. Also available as a PDF document at http://www.copyright.cornell.edu/training/copyrightterm.pdf.

[8] "§ 107. Limitations on exclusive rights: Fair use. Notwithstanding the provisions of sections 106 and 106A, the fair use of a copyrighted work, including such use by reproduction in copies or phonorecords or by any other means specified by that section, for purposes such as criticism, comment, news reporting, teaching (including multiple copies for classroom use), scholarship, or research, is not an infringement of copyright. In determining whether

If the rights metadata states that a work is unpublished, the user can assess the impact of that status on the fair use analysis.

- For works published in the United States between 1923 and 1963, renewal of the original copyright registration was required.[9] Therefore, a work published in 1945 with the correct copyright notice and registration would require a renewal of the original copyright in 1973 (1945 + 28 = 1973) in order for that copyright to be valid today. One study indicates that 15 percent or less of the works in their original copyright terms between 1923 and 1963 were renewed.[10] This means the majority of works initially protected by copyright during this period are now in the public domain. Of course, the more famous the work, the greater the likelihood that the original copyright registration was renewed. By contrast, renewals of registrations for more obscure works may be less likely.

---

the use made of a work in any particular case is a fair use the factors to be considered shall include—

(1) the purpose and character of the use, including whether such use is of a commercial nature or is for nonprofit educational purposes;

(2) the nature of the copyrighted work;

(3) the amount and substantiality of the portion used in relation to the copyrighted work as a whole; and

(4) the effect of the use upon the potential market for or value of the copyrighted work.

The fact that a work is unpublished shall not itself bar a finding of fair use if such finding is made upon consideration of all the above factors." (Emphasis added; available at http://www.copyright.gov/title17/92chap1.html#107.)

Prior to passage of the Copyright Act of 1976, fair use was based on court decisions. In 1985 the U.S. Supreme Court in *Harper & Row Publishers, Inc. v. Nation Enterprises* (471 U.S. 539) ruled on the applicability of the fair use defense to unpublished works noting the "author's right to control the first public appearance of his undisseminated expression will outweigh a claim of fair use" (p. 555). In order to clarify how the unpublished nature of a work was to be evaluated under the fair use four-factor test set forth above, and to reverse a growing presumption that fair use was not available as a defense against an infringement claim for all unpublished works, Congress passed an amendment to the law in 1992, and the last sentence of this section was added—the one in boldface above. Notwithstanding this amendment, there is general legal consensus that courts will give greater weight to the unpublished nature of the work in fair use cases than would be given if the work had already been published.

9 All terms of original copyright run through the end of the 28th calendar year, making the period for renewal registration in the above example December 31, 1973, to December 31, 1974. When checking the Copyright Office renewal records, it is advisable to look at the years immediately preceding and following the calculated year for copyright term expiration. This will ensure that the work was not renewed properly in a different year.

10 William M. Landes and Richard A. Posner, "Indefinitely Renewable Copyright," University of Chicago Law & Economics, Olin Working Paper No. 154 (August 1, 2002). http://ssm.com/abstract=319321.

- Creation date may determine when the copyright term begins and ends; it is especially important when the author is unknown, the work is a work made for hire, or the work is one of corporate authorship, that is, a work created by a company such as a movie studio or record company.
- In 2006 the U.S. Copyright Office issued its report on orphan works.[11] Later that year, hearings on orphan works were held in both the U.S. House of Representatives and the U.S. Senate, and legislation amending the Copyright Act to reduce the legal liabilities relating to use of orphan works was introduced in the U.S. House of Representatives. While this legislation did not pass, many experts think that orphan works legislation will be enacted in the next few years. If so, the hope is that penalties and remedies for use of orphan works will be reduced or eliminated altogether. For that reason, it makes sense to identify orphan works as such. Moreover, regardless of whether or not orphan work legislation passes, it seems reasonable that if an institution attempts to identify and/or locate the copyright claimant and cannot do so despite diligent efforts, and this is explained to the court, there may be some recognition of this good faith activity by the judge if an infringement claim is brought by the emergent copyright claimant.
- Prior to 1978, the law required that a copyright notice be affixed to published works. Failure to include a legally sufficient notice put in the public domain American works that were published in the United States (without the notice). Therefore, an institution may decide to classify works as in the public domain if they were purchased before January 1, 1978, or were believed to have been offered for sale to the public before that date and there is no copyright notice affixed to the work.
- Obviously, if one knows a work is in the public domain or if the institution owns the copyright, permission to use the work is not required by law, although local policy may require internal authorization.

In order for catalogers and rights metadata analysts to be able to populate the recommended rights metadata elements, the institution will need some basic rules or assumptions to apply when copyright and publication status may not be clear and some suggestions for resources to help locate the sought-after information. There are numerous recommendations for where to look for the information requested. Currently, there

---

[11] *Report on Orphan Works: A Report of the Register of Copyrights*, January 2006, United States Copyright Office. http://www.copyright.gov/orphan/.

Table 1. **Example of Core Elements for Rights Metadata**

Metadata Element	Valid Data Values for This Element	Example—Public Domain Work	Example—Work Not in the Public Domain
Title	The data values for this element should be copied (preferably in an automated manner) from the title element from the descriptive metadata record for the work or item. Per *Cataloging Cultural Objects*, this element, which is repeatable, can contain translated titles, brief titles, display titles, etc., in addition to the title that is inscribed on the item or object, if one exists. Include a subelement for the parent object/work ("title larger entity") when applicable.	*Puzza in the Likeness of Isis, Seated on a Lotus Flower/Puzza sous une forme parallele à Isis, assise sur la fleur de lotos* from *Cérémonies et coutumes religieuses de tous les peuples du monde*	*San Diego Stadium (San Diego, California)* from *Julius Shulman photography archive*
Creator	The name of the creator of the original object or work, taken from a published controlled vocabulary (e.g., LCNAF, LCSH, ULAN) or local authority file whenever possible.	*Picart, Bernard*	*Shulman, Julius*
	The life dates in the case of individual creators, including the death date if applicable. Dates should be expressed according to a standard format, e.g., ISO 8601.	*b. 1673-11-06* *d. 1733-08-05*	*b. 1910*
Creation Dates	The date(s) of the creation of the work.* Dates should be expressed according to a standard format, e.g., ISO 8601.	*1723–1743*	*1967*
Creator Nationality	The nationality or culture of the creator of the work, if known	*French*	*American*
Copyright Status	Valid values for this element should be selected from a controlled list, e.g.: • Copyright owned by the institution that holds the original object/work or item • Copyright owned by a third party—Include a subelement for the name of the third party, taken from a published controlled vocabulary whenever possible. • Public domain • Orphan work • Not yet researched	*public domain*	*copyright owned by institution* *© J. Paul Getty Trust*
Publication Status	Valid values for this element should be selected from a controlled list, e.g.: • Published—Include a subelement with the date of publication, if known, in a standard format, e.g., ISO 8601. Note that date of creation and date of publication are not necessarily identical. • Unpublished (in which case, the creator dates and/or date of creation are extremely important) • Unknown, after research and due diligence • Not yet researched	*published* *1723–1743*	*not researched*
Date of Rights Metadata Research	This should be a repeating element, since metadata research is often necessarily an incremental process to which more than one individual contributes. The individual's name or initials should be provided by the information system, and associated with the relevant dates of research. Dates should be expressed according to a standard format, e.g., ISO 8601.	*2008-10-07 MTW*	*2007-09-13 MTW*

* Note that under current U.S. copyright law, a work is protected for the life of an individual author/creator plus 70 years regardless of the date of creation. The copyright term for corporate works and works made for hire is 125 years from the date of creation, or 95 years from the date of publication.

is no resource that sets forth commonly accepted practices regarding what is legally reasonable to assume about copyright or publication when only limited information is available, so institutions will need to draft their own guidelines.[12] Of course, local policy regarding use of material presumed to be protected by copyright and the institution's risk tolerance for infringement claims that arise in case the assumption is wrong will govern use decisions.[13] With a little effort, however, the basic information needed to make informed decisions about rights for many works in an institution's collections can be easily available and accessible if the suggested rights information is captured.

Any rights metadata effort should be viewed as dynamic and ongoing. New information may come from various sources: a user, a curator, a librarian, or even the creator of the work. Rights information needs to be updated and augmented, and additional information will need to be captured for works with more complicated rights situations, such as audiovisual materials. Therefore, it is important that staff tasked with inputting rights metadata be identified to all those involved in cataloging and digitization efforts so that when new rights information is discovered, it can be input into the institutional database.

Now is the time to get started and not to be overwhelmed. Rights metadata can be made simple if everyone in the institution is aware of its long-term importance and there is a concerted, coordinated effort to research it, record it according to standards and best practices, and share it in fulfillment of the institution's mission in the digital age.

Author's Note

The rights metadata proposal and examples provided here are not legal advice. To answer specific questions of law or address policy matters with legal implications, professional advice from an attorney is always recommended.

---

[12] Drafting the assumptions to be applied locally should not be used as an excuse to delay capturing rights metadata. If necessary, institutions can start with the rights information that is known and agree on the assumptions over time.

[13] Institutions may have zero risk tolerance or may have collections consisting primarily of works by living artists. In either case, local policy may be to seek permission. Others may feel that the good faith judgment based on reasonable assumptions applied to the law and the facts is sufficient to allow use and defend in cases of infringement claims.

Practical Principles for Metadata Creation and Maintenance

1. Metadata creation is one of the core activities of collecting and memory institutions. Quality metadata creation is just as important as the care, preservation, display, and dissemination of collections; adequate planning and resources must be devoted to this ongoing, mission-critical activity.

2. Metadata creation is an incremental process and should be a shared responsibility. A metadata record may begin its life cycle as a "place holder" consisting of core data and then be enriched as it moves through the various stages of its use within an institution. By the same token, metadata creation and management should be a shared responsibility, distributed in a practical, reasonable way throughout the appropriate units of an institution, including but not limited to staff in acquisitions, cataloging and processing units, the registrar's office, digital asset management units, digitizing units, and conservation and curatorial departments. "Ad hoc" user-created metadata may be generated from work done by visiting researchers and scholars as well as other users, including nonexpert users.

3. Metadata rules and processes must be enforced in all appropriate units of an institution. Inefficiencies, gaps in mission-critical metadata, poor-quality metadata, and negative "downstream" effects on metadata creation and work flow can be avoided by establishing and enforcing processes and procedures in all the participating units throughout an institution.

4. Adequate, carefully thought-out staffing levels including appropriate skill sets are essential for the successful implementation of a cohesive, comprehensive metadata strategy. An adequate number of appropriately trained staff with a variety of expertises and skill sets (e.g., subject expertise, cataloging experience, technical knowledge, research skills, knowledge of rights issues) is necessary for implementation of a successful, institution-wide metadata strategy.

5. Institutions must build heritability of metadata into core information systems. To avoid redundant data entry and lack of synchronization of metadata in core enterprise systems and to ensure sharing of reliable, mission-critical information among the relevant units throughout the institution, interoperability for the automated transfer and validation of metadata from one core system to another must be achieved.

6. There is no "one-size-fits-all" metadata schema or controlled vocabulary or data content (cataloging) standard. Institutions must carefully choose the appropriate suite of metadata schemas and controlled vocabularies (including collection-specific thesauri and local picklists), along with the most appropriate cataloging standards (including local cataloging guidelines based on published standards) to best describe and provide access to their collections and other resources.

7. Institutions must streamline metadata production and replace manual methods of metadata creation with "industrial" production methods wherever possible and appropriate. Time- and labor-intensive procedures for metadata creation should be evaluated and streamlined wherever possible (e.g., creation of core records rather than exhaustive records; metadata work and vocabulary control focused on a very few core elements or access points; elimination of redundant and outdated work flows). Automated tools (e.g., use of templates, picklists, built-in thesauri, automated metadata generation or metadata mining) should be carefully researched and implemented as appropriate.

8. Institutions should make the creation of shareable, repurposable metadata a routine part of their work flow. Creation of consistent, standards-based, continuously refreshed and updated metadata enables institutions to publish information about their collections and other resources and activities in a timely, efficient manner and to more broadly disseminate that information through union catalogs and other "federated" resources via protocols such as the Protocol for Metadata Harvesting (OAI-PMH).

9. Research and documentation of rights metadata must be an integral part of an institution's metadata workflow. This metadata should be captured and managed in an appropriate information system that is available to the all of the individuals in the organization who need to contribute to it, as well as those who need to use it. (See "Rights Metadata Made Simple," p. 63.)

10. A high-level understanding of the importance of metadata and buy-in from upper management are essential for the successful implementation of a metadata strategy. Without a general understanding of principles 1–9 above on the part of the decision makers of an institution, it will be difficult if not impossible consistently to create adequate, appropriate metadata to enable access and use by core constituents (including internal users, the general public, and expert reseachers).

Glossary

AACR (*Anglo-American Cataloguing Rules*)
A data content standard for describing bibliographic materials. http://www.aacr2.org/.

algorithm
A formula or procedure for solving a problem or carrying out a task. An algorithm is a set of steps in a very specific order, such as a mathematical formula or the instructions in a computer program.

application profile
A set of metadata elements, policies, and guidelines defined for a particular application or community. The elements may be from one or more element sets, thus allowing a given application to meet its functional requirements by using metadata from several element sets, including locally defined elements.

authentication
A human or machine process that verifies that an individual, computer, or information object is who or what it purports to be.

authority file
A file, typically electronic, that serves as a source of standardized forms of names, terms, titles, and so on. Authority files should include references or links from variant forms to preferred forms. For example, in the Library of Congress Name Authority File (LCNAF), "Schiavone, Andrea" is the preferred name form for a Dalmatian artist active in Italy during the sixteenth century, while "Medulić, Andrija," "Lo Schiavone," and several other forms are listed as variant names. Authority files regulate usage but also provide additional access points, thus increasing both the precision and the recall of many searches.

back-end database
A database that contains and manages data for an information system, distinct from the presentation or interface components of that system.

CCO (Cataloging Cultural Objects)
A data content standard for describing works of art, architecture, and material culture.
http://www.vraweb.org/ccoweb/cco/index.html.

CDWA (*Categories for the Description of Works of Art*)
A set of metadata categories and recommendations that may be used to design information systems and to do cataloging for art, architecture, objects of material culture, and archaeological and archival materials. http://www.getty.edu/research/conducting_research/standards/cdwa/.

CDWA Lite
An XML schema for core records for art, architecture, and material culture designed to work with the OAI-PMH; the elements are based on a subset of the full element set of *Categories for the Description of Works of Art* (CDWA). http://www.getty.edu/research/conducting_research/standards/cdwa/cdwalite.html.

CGI script
A computer program, most frequently written in C, Perl, or a shell script, that uses the Common Gateway Interface (CGI) standard and provides an interactive interface between a user or an external computer application and a World Wide Web server. CGI scripts are most commonly used to develop forms that allow users to submit information to a Web server.

CIDOC CRM (CIDOC Conceptual Reference Model)
An object-oriented ontology for the mediation and interchange of hetero-geneous cultural heritage information. http://cidoc.ics.forth.gr/.

client
An application that retrieves and/or renders resources or resource manifestations. Often used to denote a computer or other kinds of devices connected to a network, equipped with software that enables users to access resources available on another computer connected to the same network, called a server. *See also* **server**.

conceptual data model
An abstract model or representation of data for a particular domain, business enterprise, field of study, etc., independent of any specific software or information system. Usually expressed in terms of entities and relationships. *See also* **logical data model**.

crosswalk
A chart or table (visual or virtual) that represents the semantic mapping of fields or data elements in one data standard to fields or data elements in another standard that has a similar function or meaning. Crosswalks make it possible to convert data between databases that use different metadata schemes and enable heterogeneous databases to be searched simultaneously with a single query as if they were a single database (semantic interoperability). Also known as field mapping. *See also* **metadata mapping**.

DACS (Describing Archives: A Content Standard)
A data content standard for describing archival collections. http://www.archivists.org/catalog/pubDetail.asp?objectID=1279.

data content standard
Rules that determine the vocabulary, syntax, or format of content entered into data fields or metadata elements, for

Many thanks to Marcia Lei Zeng of the School of Library and Information Science at Kent State University, who reviewed the glossary and provided extremely valuable input.

example, *Anglo-American Cataloguing Rules* (AACR), ISO 8601 (rules for recording date and time), *Describing Archives: A Content Standard* (DACS), *Cataloging Cultural Objects* (CCO).

data provider (OAI nomenclature)
An organization that exposes metadata records in one or more repositories (specially configured servers) for harvesting by service providers.

Deep Web
See **Hidden Web**.

default values
Values that are assumed or supplied automatically, for example, by a computer system, if a value is not specified.

digital signatures
A form of electronic authentication of a digital document. Digital signatures are created and verified using public key cryptography and serve to tie the document being signed to the signer.

digital surrogate
A digital "copy" of an original work or item, for example, a JPEG or TIFF image of a painting or sculpture or a PDF file of an article or book. In OAI nomenclature, digital surrogates are often referred to as "resources."

DTD (Document Type Definition)
A collection of markup declarations that define the structure, elements, and attributes that can be used in encoding certain type of documents in SGML or, more commonly, in XML. Examples of DTDs include the EAD DTD, the HTML DTD, and the TEI DTD. XML DTDs are gradually being replaced by the newer **XML schemas**.

Dublin Core Metadata Element Set (DCMES)
A set of 15 metadata elements that can be assigned to information resources, optimized for resource discovery on the World Wide Web. Also often used as a "lowest common denominator" in metadata mapping. http://dublincore .org/documents/dces/.

dynamically generated
Refers to a Web page, metadata record, or other information object that is generated on demand, typically from content stored in a database, and usually either in response to a user's input or from dynamic data sources that are refreshed periodically. The expression "on the fly" is often used in relation to dynamically generated content.

EAD (Encoded Archival Description)
A data structure standard for encoding archival finding aids in SGML or XML according to the EAD DTD or EAD XML schema, making it possible for the semantic contents of a hierarchically structured finding aid to be machine processed. http://www.loc.gov/ead/.

encryption
An encoding mechanism used to prevent nonauthorized users from reading digital information and also for user and document authentication. Only designated users or recipients have the capability to decode encrypted materials.

entity-relationship model
A type of conceptual data model that represents structured data in terms of entities and relationships. An entity-relationship diagram can be used to represent information objects and their relationships visually. Because the constructs used in the entity-relationship model can easily be transformed into relational tables, this type of model is often used in database design.

EXIF (Exchangeable Image File Format)
A specification for an image file format for digital cameras that provides the ability to attach image metadata to JPEG, TIFF, and RIFF images. As of this writing, EXIF is not maintained by any industry or standards organization but is widely used by camera manufacturers. http:// www.exif.org/.

field mapping
See **crosswalk**.

FTP (File Transfer Protocol)
A TCP/IP protocol that allows data files to be copied directly from one computer to another over the Internet.

finding aid
A descriptive tool widely used in archives. Finding aids typically take the form of hierarchical narrative descriptions of cohesive groups of archival records or collections of manuscript materials. Finding aids traditionally were paper documents; EAD is a structured way of expressing finding aids as machine-readable data.

FRBR (Functional Requirements for Bibliographic Records)
A set of requirements and a conceptual entity-relationship model developed by the International Federation of Library Associations and Institutions (IFLA) to support bibliographic access and control. http://www.ifla.org/VII/s13/frbr/frbr.htm.

FRBRoo
A joint initiative of the International Federation of Library Associations and Institutions (IFLA) and the International Council of Museums–International Documentation Committee (ICOM-CIDOC) to create an object-oriented ontology that both captures the semantics of bibliographic information and harmonizes those concepts in common with the CIDOC CRM, thus facilitating information interchange between the museum and library communities. http://cidoc.ics .forth.gr/frbr_inro.html.

folksonomy
An assemblage of concepts, represented by terms and names (called "tags"), the result of social tagging. Note that a folksonomy is not a true taxonomy. *See also* **social tagging**, **taxonomy**.

Google Sitemap
Metadata about the content of a Web site that assists the Googlebot Web crawler to index a site more efficiently and comprehensively. www.google .com/webmasters/sitemaps/.

granularity

The level of detail at which an information object or resource is viewed or described.

harvester (OAI nomenclature)

A computer system that sends OAI-PMH requests to OAI data providers' repositories and harvests metadata records from them.

header metadata

Metadata embedded in the header part of a digital file.

Hidden Web (also known as Deep Web, Invisible Web)

The sum of the Web pages that are not accessible to Web crawlers, usually because they are either dynamically generated by a user querying a database or password-protected or subscription-based.

hostname

An identifier for a specific machine on the Internet. The hostname identifies not only the machine but also its subnet and domain, for example, www.getty.edu. *See also* **domain name**.

HTML (HyperText Markup Language)

An SGML-derived markup language used to create documents for World Wide Web applications. HTML has evolved to emphasize design and appearance rather than the representation of document structure and metadata elements.

HTTP

HyperText Transfer Protocol, the standard protocol that enables users with Web browsers to access HTML documents and related media.

hyperlink

An abbreviated reference to a "hypertext link," a method of creating nonlinear pathways between related digital documents or to link to related objects such as image or audio files.

information object

A digital item or group of items referred to as a unit, regardless of type or format, that a computer can address or manipulate as a single discrete object.

Internet

A global collection of computer networks that exchange information by the TCP/IP suite of networking protocols.

Internet directory

A thematically organized list of descriptive links to Internet sites, often created by humans who have classified sites by their content. Yahoo! provides numerous such directories.

interoperability

The ability of different information systems to work together, particularly in the correct interpretation of data semantics and functionality. *See also* **semantic interoperability**.

Invisible Web

See **Hidden Web**.

legacy system

An information system that has been developed and modified over a period of time and has become outdated and difficult and costly to maintain but that holds important information and involves processes that are deeply ingrained in an organization. Legacy systems usually are eventually replaced by a new hardware and software configuration.

link resolver

Software that uses the OpenURL standard to automatically redirect a user's request to the most appropriate copy of a networked digital object. Typically, link resolvers are used by libraries to direct their patrons from bibliographic records or abstracts to licensed subscription-based resources such as full-text electronic versions of articles and books. http://www.niso.org/standards/standard_detail.cfm?std_id=783.

logical data model

A data model that includes all entities and the relationships among them based on the structures identified in a conceptual data model and that specifies all attributes for each entity. The data is described in as much detail as possible, without regard to how it will be physically implemented in a specific database.

MARC (Machine-Readable Cataloging format)

A set of standardized data structures for describing bibliographic materials that facilitates cooperative cataloging and data exchange in bibliographic information systems. http://www.loc.gov/marc/.

markup language

A formal way of annotating a document or collection of digital data using embedded encoding tags to indicate the structure of the document or datafile and the contents of its data elements. This markup also provides a computer with information about how to process and display marked-up documents. HTML, XML, and SGML are examples of standardized markup languages.

memory institution

A generic term used to describe an institution that has a responsibility to collect, care for, and provide access to the human record—for example, museums, libraries, and archives.

metadata mapping

A formal identification of equivalent or nearly equivalent metadata elements or groups of metadata elements within different metadata schemas, carried out in order to facilitate semantic interoperability.

metadata mining

The automated extraction of metadata from electronic documents.

metasearch

Searching of diverse databases on diverse platforms with diverse metadata in real time by means of one or more protocols. The NISO MetaSearch Initiative defines metasearch as "search and retrieval to span multiple databases, sources, platforms, protocols, and vendors at once." Metasearch enables users to enter search criteria once and access several search engines simultaneously. With metasearch, fresh records are always available, because searching is in real time, in a distributed environment. http://www.niso.org/committees/MS_initiative.html.

META tag
An HTML tag that enables metadata to be embedded invisibly on Web pages, for example, Description, Keywords.

META tag spamming
The deliberate misuse of meta tags in order to attract traffic to a site, for example, by boosting its ranking in search results.

METS (Metadata Encoding Transmission Schema)
A standard for encoding descriptive, administrative, and structural metadata relating to objects in a digital library, expressed in XML. METS enables the "packaging" of complex digital objects that include a range of metadata as well as related digital surrogates. http://www .loc.gov/standards/mets/

MODS (Metadata Object Description Schema)
An XML schema for bibliographic records, developed and maintained by the Library of Congress. http://www .loc.gov/standards/mods/.

namespace
The set of unique names used to identify objects within a well-defined domain, particularly relevant for XML applications. An XML Namespace is a W3C recommendation for providing uniquely named elements and attributes in an XML instance. A namespace is declared using the reserved XML attribute xmlns, the value of which must be a URI (Uniform Resource Identifier) reference. For example, the Dublin Core Metadata Element Set, Version 1.1 (original 15 elements) has the approved DCMI namespace URI as http://purl. org/dc/elements/1.1/.

nesting
The way in which subelements may be contained within larger elements, resulting in multiple levels of metadata.

network bandwidth
Derived from the term used to describe the size or "width" of the frequencies used to carry analog communications such as television and radio. For Internet

purposes, bandwidth is generally (and incorrectly) used to refer to the rate of data transfer.

OAI-PMH (Open Archives Initiative Protocol for Metadata Harvesting)
A protocol used to harvest or collect metadata records from data providers. http://www.openarchives.org/pmh/.

object-oriented
A programming or data modeling methodology that utilizes the notion of classes and their properties. Members (or instances) of a class share the same properties—for example, color or weight (however, note that although members of a class all share the same properties, the values of those properties do not need to be the same). Classes can contain subclasses, members of which inherit the properties of the parent or "superclass."

ontology
A formal, machine-readable specification of a conceptual model, in which concepts, properties, relationships, functions, constraints, and axioms are all explicitly defined.

OPAC (Online Public Access Catalog)
A computerized inventory of a library's holdings.

Open WorldCat
A subset of the WorldCat union bibliographic database made available by OCLC to certain Web search engines and online book retailers. http://www.oclc .org/worldcat/open/.

PageRank™ (Google)
A proprietary link-analysis algorithm developed by Google founders Larry Page and Sergey Brin to assign a numerical score to each document in a set of hypertext documents based on the number of referring links. The algorithm also takes into account the rank of the referring page, such that a link from a high-ranking page counts more than a link from a low-ranking page. http://www.google .com/technology/.

precision
A measure of search effectiveness expressed as the ratio of relevant records or documents retrieved from a database to the total number retrieved in response to the query; for example, in a database containing 100 records relevant to the topic "book history," a search retrieving 50 records, 25 of which are relevant to the topic, would have 50 percent precision (25/50). (Definition from ODLIS, *Online Dictionary for Library and Information Science*, http://lu.com/odlis/.) *See also* **recall**.

protocol
A specification—often a standard—that describes how computers communicate with each other, for example, the TCP/IP suite of communication protocols or the OAI-PMH.

RDF (Resource Description Framework)
An application of XML that enables the creation of rich, structured, machine-readable resource descriptions. http:// www.w3.org/RDF/.

RDF schema
A set of semantics within a defined namespace for use with specific applications of RDF.

recall
A measure of the effectiveness of a search expressed as the ratio of the number of relevant records or documents retrieved in response to the query to the total number of relevant records or documents in the database; for example, in a database containing 100 records relevant to the topic "book history," a search retrieving 50 records, 25 of which are relevant to the topic, would have 25 percent recall (25/100). (Definition from ODLIS, *Online Dictionary for Library and Information Science*, http://lu.com/ odlis/.) *See also* **precision**.

relevance
The extent to which information retrieved in a search of a library collection or other resource, such as an online catalog or a bibliographic database, is judged by the user to be applicable to ("about") the

subject of the query. Relevance depends on the searcher's subjective perception of the degree to which the document fulfills the information need, which may or may not have been expressed fully or with precision in the search statement. Measures of the effectiveness of information retrieval, such as precision and recall, depend on the relevance of search results. (Definition from ODLIS, *Online Dictionary for Library and Information Science*, http://lu.com/odlis/.)

relevance ranking

The algorithmic process, a feature of many search software applications, by which results in a result set are sorted or ranked according to their relevance. In OPACs, for example, relevance is computed based upon the number of occurrences of the search term in the record that is retrieved, and the weight assigned to the field(s) in which the search term appears. (Definition from ODLIS, *Online Dictionary for Library and Information Science*, http://lu.com/odlis/.) Google's PageRank™ is an example of a relevance ranking algorithm.

resource discovery

The process of searching for specific information objects on the Web.

robot

See **Web crawler**.

schema

A set of rules for encoding information that supports specific communities of users. Also called "scheme." The plural forms of the word *schema* are *schemas* and *schemata*. *See also* **XML schema**.

schema registry

An authoritative source of names, semantics, and syntaxes for one or more schemas.

screen scraping

A technique in which display data (usually unstructured) is automatically retrieved and extracted, for example, from a Web page.

search engine

A computer program that allows users to search electronic resources. In the context of the World Wide Web, the term usually refers to a program that searches a large index of Web pages generated by an automated Web crawler. *See also* **Web search engine**.

semantic interoperability

The ability of different agents, services, and applications to communicate data while ensuring accuracy and preserving the meaning of the data (definition based on Marcia Bates and Mary Niles Maack, *Encyclopedia of Library and Information Sciences*, 3rd ed. [New York: Marcel Dekker, forthcoming]).

Semantic Web

An evolving, collaborative effort led by the W3C whose goal is to provide a common framework that will allow data to be shared and re-used across various applications as well as across enterprise and community boundaries. It derives from W3C director and inventor of the World Wide Web Sir Tim Berners-Lee's vision of the Web as a universal medium for data, information, and knowledge exchange.

server

An application that supplies resources or resource manifestations. Often used to refer to a networked computer that acts as a source of data and/or applications used by multiple client computers or devices. *See also* **client**.

service provider (OAI nomenclature)

An institution or organization that harvests metadata from data providers and uses the aggregated metadata as a basis for building value-added services.

SGML (Standard Generalized Markup Language)

International Standards Organization standard ISO/IEC 8879:1986; a markup language first used by the publishing industry, for defining, specifying, and creating digital documents that can be delivered, displayed, linked, and manipulated in a system-independent manner. XML and HTML are derived from SGML.

social bookmarking

The decentralized practice and method by which individuals and groups create, classify, store, discover, and share Web bookmarks or "favorites" in an online "social" environment.

social tagging

The decentralized practice and method by which individuals and groups create, manage, and share terms, names, and so on (called tags), to annotate and categorize digital resources in an online "social" environment. A folksonomy is the result of social tagging. Also referred to as collaborative tagging, social classification, social indexing, mob indexing, folk categorization. *See also* **folksonomy**, **tagging**.

spamming

Used in reference to meta tags. The abuse of metadata that creators include in the HTML header area of their Web pages in order to increase the number of visitors to a Web site. Keyword spamming entails repeating keywords multiple times in order to appear at the top of search engine result listings or listing keywords that are irrelevant to the site in order to attract visitors under false pretenses.

spider

See **Web crawler**.

SRU/SRW (Search and Retrieve via URL/Search and Retrieve Web Service)

Companion protocols for Web search queries utilizing the CQL Common Query Language. http://www.loc .gov/standards/sru/.

surrogate

See **digital surrogate**.

tagging

In the context of the Web, the act of associating terms (called tags) with an information object (e.g., a Web page, an image, a streaming video clip), thus describing the item and enabling keyword-based classification and retrieval. Tags—a form of user-generated metadata—from communities of users can be aggregated and analyzed, providing useful information about the collection of objects with which the tags have been associated. *See also* **social tagging**.

taxonomy
An orderly classification that explicitly expresses the relationships, usually hierarchical (e.g., genus/species, whole/part, class/instance), between and among the things being classified.

TCP/IP (Transmission Control Protocol/ Internet Protocol)
The ISO standardized suite of network protocols that enables information systems to communicate with other information systems on the Internet, regardless of their computer platforms.

TEI (Text Encoding Initiative)
An international cooperative effort to develop guidelines for standard encoding schemes (i.e., the TEI and TEI Lite DTDs) for literary and linguistic texts. http://www.tei-c.org/.

URI (Uniform Resource Identifier)
A short string that uniquely identifies a resource such as an HTML document, an image, a downloadable file, or a service. URLs and URNs are types of URIs.

URL (Uniform Resource Locator)
A type of URI consisting of an Internet address that tells users how and where to locate a specific file on the World Wide Web. A URL includes not only the name of a file but also the name of the host computer, the directory path to get to that file, and the protocol needed in order to use it (e.g., http://www.getty.edu/research/conducting_research/standards/intrometadata/intro.html specifies that the hypertext transfer protocol "http" should be used to retrieve the document intro.html from the host www.getty.edu in the directory research/conducting_research/standards/intrometadata.

URN (Uniform Resource Name)
A type of URI consisting of a unique, location-independent identifier of a file available on the Internet. The file remains accessible by its URN regardless of changes that might occur in its

host and directory path. For example, urn:issn:0167-6423 is the URN for the journal *Science of Computer Programming*.

Visible Web
The subset of the World Wide Web that is visible to Web browsers and indexable by search engines' Web crawlers. To be accessible to Web crawlers, the pages must be accessible simply by following links (i.e., not generated dynamically in response to user input) and not protected by a password.

VRA Core 4.0
An XML schema for describing works of art and architecture and their visual surrogates. http://www.vraweb.org/projects/vracore4/index.html

W3C (World Wide Web Consortium)
The main international standards organization for the World Wide Web.

Web 2.0
A phrase used loosely by the Web development community to refer to a perceived "second generation" of Web technologies and applications. Wikis, folksonomies, gaming, podcasting, blogging, and so on, are all considered Web 2.0 applications.

Web browser
A software application that enables users to view and interact with information and media files on the Web. Internet Explorer, Mozilla Firefox, and Netscape Navigator are examples of Web browsers.

Web crawler (robot, spider)
A software program that systematically traverses the Web, either for the purpose of generating a searchable index of Web content or to gather statistics.

Web server
A computer that is able to respond to HTTP requests from clients known as Web browsers and return the appropriate HTTP responses—most typically serving an HTML page.

Web search engine/Internet search engine
A software program that collects data taken from the content of files available

on the Web and puts them in an index or database that Web users can search in a variety of ways. The search results provide links back to the pages matching the user's search in their original location.

wiki
A collaborative Web site that contains pages that any authorized user can edit. Wikis typically retain all former versions of each page, allowing the revision history of a page to be tracked and for unwanted revisions to be reversed.

Wikipedia
A free, collaborative, volunteer-driven Web-based encyclopedia that utilizes wiki software to allow anyone to edit articles. http://en.wikipedia.org/wiki/.

World Wide Web
A vast distributed wide-area client-server architecture for retrieving hypermedia documents over the Internet.

XHTML (Extensible HyperText Markup Language)
A reformulation of HTML in XML.

XML (Extensible Markup Language)
A simple, flexible markup language derived from SGML. Originally designed for large-scale electronic publishing, XML is now playing an increasingly important role in the publication and exchange of a wide variety of data on the Web.

XML schema
A machine-readable definition of the structure, elements, and attributes allowed in a valid instance of a conforming XML document. XML schemas are expressed using the XML Schema Definition language, a W3C standard. http://www.w3.org/TR/xmlschema-0/.

XMP (Extensible Metadata Platform)
A markup language, based on RDF, for recording and embedding metadata about digital assets. Developed by Adobe Systems and supported across the company's range of software products

and file formats. http://www.adobe.com/products/xmp/index.html.

Z39.50

An ISO 23950 and ANSI/NISO Z39.50 standard information retrieval protocol. Z39.50 is a client/server-based protocol for searching and retrieving information from remote databases.

Selected Bibiography

Metadata: General

California Digital Library Services Advisory Group. *CDL Guidelines for Digital Objects*. Version 2.0. (June 2007). Reviewed and updated annually. Available at http://www.cdlib.org/inside/diglib/guidelines.

Caplan, Priscilla. *Metadata Fundamentals for All Librarians*. Chicago: American Library Association, 2003.

Cole, Timothy W., and Muriel Foulonneau. *Using the Open Archives Initiative Protocol for Metadata Harvesting*. Westport, CT: Libraries Unlimited, 2007. Table of contents available at http://www.loc.gov/catdir/toc/ecip0714/2007009006.html.

Haynes, David. *Metadata for Information Management and Retrieval*. London: Library Association Publishing, 2004.

Hillmann, Diane I., and Elaine L. Westbrocks, eds. *Metadata in Practice*. Chicago: American Library Association, 2004.

Intner, Sheila, Susan S. Lazinger, and Jean Weihs. *Metadata and Its Impact on Libraries*. Westport, CT: Libraries Unlimited, 2006.

National Information Standards Organization. *Understanding Metadata*. Bethesda, MD: NISO Press, 2004. Available at http://www.niso.org/standards/ resources/ UnderstandingMetadata.pdf.

Shreeves, Sarah L., et al. "Is 'Quality' Metadata 'Shareable' Metadata? The Implications of Local Metadata Practices for Federated Collections." In *Proceedings of the Twelfth National Conference of the Association of College and Research Libraries, April 7–10, Minneapolis, MN*, ed. H. A. Thompson, pp. 223–37. Chicago: ACRL, 2005.

Taylor, Arlene G., with Daniel N. Joudrey. *The Organization of Information*. 3rd ed. Westport, CT: Libraries Unlimited, 2008.

Metadata: Specific Standards

Baca, Murtha, et al. *Cataloging Cultural Objects: A Guide to Describing Cultural Works and Their Images*. Chicago: American Library Association, 2006.

Crofts, Nick, Martin Doerr, Tony Gill, Stephen Stead, and Matthew Stiff, eds. *Definition of the CIDOC Conceptual Reference Model*, ICOM/CIDOC CRM Special Interest Group, 2005. Available at http://cidoc.ics.forth.gr/docs/cidoc_crm_version_4.2.pdf.

Gorman, Michael, and Paul W. Winkler. *Anglo-American Cataloguing Rules*. 2nd ed., 1998 rev. Chicago: American Library Association, 1998.

Hillmann, Diane I. *Using Dublin Core* (2005). http://dublincore.org/documents/usageguide/.

IFLA Study Group on the Functional Requirements for Bibliographic Records. *Functional Requirements for Bibliographic Records: Final Report*. Munich: K. G. Saur, 1998. Available at http://www.ifla.org/VII/s13/frbr/frbr.pdf.

Pitti, Daniel V., and Wendy Duff, eds. *Encoded Archival Description on the Internet*. Binghamton, NY: Haworth Information Press, 2002.

Roe, Kathleen D. *Arranging and Describing Archives and Manuscripts (Archival Fundamentals Series II)*. Chicago: Society of American Archivists, 2005.

Society of American Archivists. *Describing Archives: A Content Standard*. Chicago: Society of American Archivists, 2005.

On Digital Projects

Besser, Howard. *Introduction to Imaging*. Revised edition edited by Sally Hubbard with Deborah Lenert. Los Angeles: Getty Research Institute, 2003. Available at http://www.getty.edu/research/conducting_research/standards/introimages/.

Deegan, Marilyn, and Simon Tanner. *Digital Futures: Strategies for the Information Age*. New York: Neal Schuman, 2002.

Hughes, Lorna M. *Digitizing Collections: Strategic Issues for the Information Manager*. London: Facet, 2004.

Institute of Museum and Library Services. *NLG Project Planning: A Tutorial*. Available at http://www.imls.gov/project_planning/.

Kenney, Anne R., and Oya Y. Rieger. *Moving Theory into Practice: Digital Imaging for Libraries and Archives*. Mountain View, CA: Research Libraries Group, 2000.

———. *Moving Theory into Practice: Digital Imaging Tutorial*. Ithaca, NY: Cornell University, 2003. Available at http://www.library.cornell.edu/preservation/tutorial/index.html.

Lee, Stuart D. *Digital Imaging: A Practical Handbook*. New York: Neal-Schuman, 2001.

NISO Framework Advisory Group. *A Framework of Guidance for Building Good Digital Collections*. 3rd ed. Baltimore, MD: National Information Standards Organization, 2008. Available at http://www.niso.org/framework/framework3.pdf.

Sitts, Maxine K. *Handbook for Digital Projects: A Management Tool for Preservation and Access*. Andover, MA: Northeast Document Conservation Center, 2000. Available at http://nedcc.org/oldnedccsite/digital/dighome.htm.

Stielow, Frederick J. *Building Digital Archives, Descriptions, and Displays: A How-To-Do-It Manual for Librarians and Archivists*. New York: Neal-Schuman, 2003.

Washington State Library. *Digital Best Practices*. http://digitalwa.statelib.wa.gov/best.htm.

Contributors

Murtha Baca (mbaca@getty.edu) is Head of the Getty Vocabulary Program at the Getty Research Institute in Los Angeles. She holds a Ph.D. in art history and Italian language and literature from the University of California, Los Angeles (UCLA). She is the author of numerous articles in the field of art documentation. In addition, she is the editor of *Introduction to Art Image Access* (Getty Research Institute, 2002) and a coeditor of *Cataloging Cultural Objects: A Guide to Describing Cultural Works and Their Images* (American Library Association, 2006). Baca has taught workshops and seminars on metadata, visual resources cataloging, and thesaurus construction at museums, universities, and other organizations in North and South America and Europe; she teaches a graduate seminar on metadata in the Department of Information Studies at UCLA.

Tony Gill (tg@tonygill.com) is the Global Library Science Specialist for an advertising agency in New York. He is also an adjunct professor at New York University's Graduate School of Arts and Science, where he teaches a class on Interactive Technology in Museums as part of the Museum Studies program. Gill spent thirteen years developing collaborative, standards-based solutions for the creation and delivery of digital cultural heritage information before assuming his current position. He has degrees in communication in computing (Middlesex University) and physics and philosophy (King's College, London). He is the author of a number of publications on the use of information technology in the cultural heritage sector, including *The MDA Guide to Computers in Museums* (Museum Documentation Association, 1996), and "3-D Culture on the Web" (*RLG DigiNews* 5, no. 3 [June 2001]). He is a coauthor of the *CIDOC Conceptual Reference Model* (ISO Standard 21127:2006).

Anne J. Gilliland (gilliland@ucla.edu) is Professor of Information Studies and Moving Image Archive Studies in the Department of Information Studies at the University of California, Los Angeles (UCLA), and Director of the Center for Information as Evidence at UCLA. She holds a Ph.D. in information and library studies, with a cognate in business information systems, from the University of Michigan. Her extensive publications include *Enduring Paradigm, New Opportunities: The Value of the Archival Perspective in the Digital Environment* (Council on Library and Information Resources, 2000); and "Metadata—Where Are We Going?" in *International Yearbook of Library and Information Management 2003: Metadata Applications and Management* (Facet Publishing, 2003). Her areas of research and teaching include archives and manuscripts, multimedia information resources, management of digital records, information as evidence, and information-seeking and use.

Maureen Whalen (mwhalen@getty.edu) is Associate General Counsel at the J. Paul Getty Trust, where she works on cultural property and intellectual property matters. She received her undergraduate and law degrees from the State University of New York at Buffalo and her MLIS from the University of California, Los Angeles. Whalen is active in the Museum Attorneys Group and was a member of the Section 108 Study Group, formed to prepare findings and make recommendations to the Librarian of Congress for possible alterations to Section 108 of the Copyright Act that would take into account current technologies.

Mary S. Woodley (mary.woodley@csun.edu) received her Ph.D. from the University of California, Los Angeles, in classical archaeology and her MLIS in library science. Since 1994 she has worked professionally as a cataloger at the Getty Research Institute and at California State University, Northridge (CSUN), cataloging all formats of information resources. More recently, she has focused on cataloging digital objects using a variety of metadata standards and controlled vocabularies. She is an active member of the Dublin Core Metadata Initiative and is a member of its advisory board. Woodley is also an elected member of the Cataloging and Classification Executive Committee of the American Library Association's Association for Library Collections and Technical Services (ALCTS). She has published on digital projects and metadata and recently created a workshop on managing digital projects for ALCTS and the Library of Congress. She teaches an advanced seminar on knowledge management at CSUN.